The Best
Stage Scenes
# of 1995

Other books by Jocelyn A. Beard

100 Men's Stage Monologues from the 1980's

100 Women's Stage Monologues from the 1980's

The Best Men's/Women's Stage Monologues of 1990

The Best Men's/Women's Stage Monologues of 1991

The Best Men's/Women's Stage Monologues of 1992

The Best Men's/Women's Stage Monologues of 1993

The Best Men's/Women's Stage Monologues of 1994

The Best Stage Scenes for Men from the 1980's

The Best Stage Scenes for Women from the 1980's

The Best Stage Scenes of 1992

The Best Stage Scenes of 1993

The Best Stage Scenes of 1994

The Best Stage Scenes of 1995

Monologues from Classic Plays 468 B.C. to 1960 A.D.

Scenes from Classic Plays 468 B.C. to 1970 A.D.

100 Great Monologues from the Renaissance Theatre

100 Great Monologues from the Neo-Classical Theatre

100 Great Monologues from the 19th C. Romantic & Realistic Theatre

Smith and Kraus *Books For Actors*
SCENE STUDY SERIES
Scenes From Classic Plays 468 B.C. to 1960 A.D.

The Best Stage Scenes of 1995

The Best Stage Scenes of 1994

The Best Stage Scenes of 1993

The Best Stage Scenes of 1992

The Best Stage Scenes for Men / Women from the 1980's

THE MONOLOGUE SERIES
The Best Men's / Women's Stage Monologues of 1994

The Best Men's / Women's Stage Monologues of 1993

The Best Men's / Women's Stage Monologues of 1992

The Best Men's / Women's Stage Monologues of 1991

The Best Men's / Women's Stage Monologues of 1990

One Hundred Men's / Women's Stage Monologues from the 1980's

2 Minutes and Under: Character Monologues for Actors

Street Talk: Character Monologues for Actors

Uptown: Character Monologues for Actors

Ice Babies in Oz: Character Monologues for Actors

Monologues from Contemporary Literature: Volume I

Monologues from Classic Plays

100 Great Monologues from the Renaissance Theatre

100 Great Monologues from the Neo-Classical Theatre

100 Great Monologues from the 19th C. Romantic and Realistic Theatres

A Brave and Violent Theatre: 20th C. Irish Monologues, Scenes & Hist. Context

Kiss and Tell: Restoration Monologues, Scenes and Historical Context

The Great Monologues from the Humana Festival

The Great Monologues from the EST Marathon

The Great Monologues from the Women's Project

The Great Monologues from the Mark Taper Forum

YOUNG ACTOR SERIES
Great Scenes and Monologues for Children

Great Monologues for Young Actors

Great Scenes for Young Actors

Multicultural Monologues for Young Actors

Multicultural Scenes for Young Actors

If you require pre-publication information about upcoming Smith and Kraus books, you may receive our semi-annual catalogue, free of charge, by sending your name and address to *Smith and Kraus Catalogue, P.O. Box 127, One Main Street, Lyme, NH 03768. Or call us at (800) 895-4331, fax (603) 795-4427.*

The Best
Stage Scenes
of 1995

edited by Jocelyn A. Beard

Scene Study Series

SK
A Smith and Kraus Book

Published by Smith and Kraus, Inc.
One Main Street, Lyme, NH 03768

First Edition: March 1996
10 9 8 7 6 5 4 3 2 1

The Scene Study Series 1067-3253

NOTE: These scenes are intended to be used for audition and class study; permission is not required to use the material for those purposes. However, if there is a paid performance of any of the scenes included in this book, please refer to the permissions acknowledgment pages to locate the source who can grant permission for public performance.

Contents

Scenes for Men

Scenes for Women

Preface

1995 is the midway point in a decade that has so far proved to be defined by struggle and conflict. From Waco to Serejevo, humankind has found itself smack dab in the middle of and era of social, political and even individual unrest; and to date the greatest struggle seems to be to discover exactly what our role in the struggle should be. You will find these concepts echoed in the plays in this book, for they represent the best of a season that if anything gave a resounding voice to the global and domestic upheavals which keep the concept of struggle in the forefront of our collective mind.

In Richard Lay's *Kept Men,* we are introduced to a group of men who all struggle to maintain their sanity and self-respect after falling victim to corporate downsizing. Dusan Kovacevic's *The Professional* takes us to present day Belgrade, where two former enemies struggle to find meaning in their new lives in which they have been liberated from the yoke of communism. Two women in Elyse Nass's *Alphabet of Flowers* struggle to reveal their love for one another after 40 years spent apart. And Steve Tanenbaum's *Drive Like Jackson Pollock* tells the tale of a man's struggle against heroin addiction.

The scenes in this book are powerful; pitting character against character, and ultimately against the world and times in which we are all struggling to survive. What is a scene, after all, if not a struggle between two or more voices?

Prepare yourself.

Break a leg!

Jocelyn Beard
Patterson, NY
Winter 1996

Dedicated to: Mary Jane Phelan, Beth Bonnabeau-Harding, Fred Rueck, Scott Cox, Steve Faiella, Michele Fulves, Francis A. Daley and Christine Pennisi, who along with the Schoolhouse Theatre, helped me to realize a very important dream.

Introduction

The Best Stage Scenes of 1995? How come?

Well, to begin with, "best" scenes don't grow on trees. And that's not a bad eco-metaphor, if you think of a play as a living entity rooted in the collective consciousness of a culture and carefully pruned to mature form by the individual gardener/playwright. Some plays have "best" scenes in blossoming profusion, some never quite manage to sprout a single one. That's life in the Cosmic Pea Patch.

What should a "best" scene have? In a nutshell—everything. It should spell out the play's chief conflicts, define character essence, encapsulate thematic nuclei. It should provide emotional impact—upon actors onstage as well as viewers offstage. It should deliver an instant immersion into a world that may appear familiar, yet suddenly explode with surprise and revelation, an all-encompassing world of such convincing substance that it becomes our world...*totally* our world...the *only* world in our spellbound imaginations that there is, was or ever will be.

And the *best* of the "best" scenes possess something extra: an electric undercurrent of escalating intensity coursing throughout from the first word, the first gesture, even in the most seemingly innocuous dialogue...an intensity that builds to a dramatic flash point where the core of the play appears and utterly transfigures the moment, sometimes forcefully like a tree limb crashing through the roof—defenses collapse, facades crumble, bubbles burst, whole lifetimes of pretense peel away as characters hurtle headlong into a hurricane maelstrom of self-discovery...but more often in the subtle, ruminative manner of an unforeseen epiphany glimpsed in a twinkling out of the corner of our mind's eye—the fleeting shadow of a bird's wing silhouetted against slow-ripening leaves blushing with a last burst of color in the waning rays of autumn sunlight.

Enough already of this nature babble. For actors and directors seeking exciting new audition material, the *The Best Stage Scenes of 1995* offers a selection of the most compelling and memorable writing in contemporary theatre, pure and simple. The diversity of characters, dialects and dramatic conflicts provides a limitless canvas for interpretive nuance and experimentation. Playwrights will also find *The Best Stage Scenes of 1995* extremely enlightening, each entry a virtual mini-workshop in professional writing technique marked by sharp dialogue, vibrant action, richly drawn character relationships.

The Best Stage Scenes of 1995? A bumper crop for sure.

L.E. McCullough

L.E. McCullough, Playwright/Composer: His work includes *Blues for Miss Buttercup*; *Connlaoi's Tale*; *Buddy Lee Perriman Reflects on the Persian Gulf Crisis, Day 15, Plays of America from American Folklore for Children, Plays of America from American Folklore for Young Actors, Ice Babies in Oz: Character Monologues for Actors*

American Medea

Silas Jones

Scene: The Mt. Vernon estate of George Washington, 1700s
    1 Man and 1 Woman: Medea (50s) an African sorceress of Ethiopian descent, and Jason (30s) her husband, a Greek.

Jason has brought Medea and their two sons to America where he is convinced they will find a bright new life. They are taken in by George Washington. Medea is shocked by the subjugation of Washington's slaves and chooses to move into the slave quarters with Imhotep, her black son, while awaiting the arrival of a ship that will take her back to Colchis. Jason has allowed himself to be seduced by the promises of a fledgling democracy and has moved into the main house with Alexander, their white son. Here, Jason pays a visit to Medea and it soon becomes obvious that their love has been destroyed.

(Late afternoon. Before Jason can knock on the door of the slave cabin, Medea comes outdoors. Jason, startled by her appearance, takes a step backward. She is dressed in slave burlap and looks as if she's just gotten over a catastrophic illness.)

JASON: Medea? You look—

MEDEA: What gorgeous hunk knocketh at Medea's chambers? Wow, it's Jason, my eternally youthful little love machine.

Sit, you slut, and lie to your haggard wife.

(They sit in the two chairs facing each other.)

MEDEA: The children, are they safe?

JASON: Of course, they have the protection of the president himself. Why are you here in the slave quarters dressed like a common slave?

MEDEA: While in Rome…I promised to stay in my place.

JASON: Good. Let's keep him in a generous mood. He's grown very fond of Alexander, you know.

MEDEA: That's goddamn white of him. Oh I've seen him prancing about the courtyard on his milk-white steed—a petty-perfect little gentleman.

JASON: Generals do that. Prance about on their steeds.

MEDEA: Like a homespun Caesar, surveying his kingdom, his African chattel.

JASON: Bitter still, are you? Be grateful Medea, he's letting you and the boys go home. He's not afraid of you you know. He could have—

MEDEA: Medea thanks Jason for his divine intervention. Jason, America's pin-up patron saint. I hear he's declared you a national treasure. You two make a classical pair. You'll go far. Too bad he's sold his half-breed daughters to the highest bidders. But then, he didn't know that Jason the Greek prefers dark meat.

JASON: Your tongue will be your death. Be happy for me, Medea.

MEDEA: Happy? The slave should be happy for the master? Yes. This place is pregnant with paradox. Irony rocks its cradle. The slave women suckle their master's children. Did you know that? They grow their own masters. The milk of Africa flows in the masters' bones yet they pay homage to Greece. Don't you find that ironic, Jason?

JASON: I thought I had seen all of your dark moods, but this one…You're beginning to look like Medusa. I don't like it. You've changed.

MEDEA: Yes, I *have* been feeling a little African lately.

JASON: And I American. Be happy for me, Medea. You can't imagine how good it is to be a citizen again. To belong. Have roots. *(Beat.)* Oh stop looking at me like that. Let's face it, you could never belong here, Medea. Your past, your heritage, your culture—the old gods are dead, the golden age of Ethiopia has ended. Medea, accept your fate. Say good-bye to Africa. Let her drown in her own tears.

MEDEA: But Africa shall rise again, Jason. Not soon, no. Four centuries from now, She shall rise. I have seen this. I have seen the future.

JASON: Let's not talk history, Medea. We've been through hell together, and now it's time to say good-bye. I know you still love me but—

MEDEA: I've laid my love to rest, Jason. My well-licked wounds have healed. This place has made me realize that we, too, were alone, Jason, in our togetherness, our yours-and-mine togetherness.

JASON: You still love me. It's all right, admit it.

MEDEA: Beware Jason. To a royal sorceress love is the eyes in the back of hate's head. The world has kicked me out. It's time for a new myth, a new tragedy. Let us say farewell and accept our fate.

JASON: America is my fate, and loving Jason is Medea's.

MEDEA: No, Jason, that's your version, the tragic Greek version. Get it through your head: Medea the African no longer loves Jason the Greek. *(Beat.)* You wonder why I'm here, dressed like a common slave. Don't you feel it? I *am* a slave Jason, so long as I reside here. Something's draining me. I feel this god's handiwork. He's dividing this people…branding them with color-coded destinies.

JASON: Nonsense. Witch talk. I still love you, Medea.

MEDEA: Careful Jason, I'm weening my powers. You never loved me, Jason, you loved the Golden Fleece. Aunt Circe warned me: Beware of Gifts bearing Greeks. The womb of a royal sorceress is sacred. I opened my legs to life and the rest is history. And for this Medea now breaks bread with Silence. *(Beat.)* When does my ship sail, Jason? A week has passed already. I fear for the children. When?

JASON: He said soon.

MEDEA: Soon? Tell him how dangerous Medea is when she's suspicious! There, I felt him!…watching me…He's both male and female…of royal birth…He knows of my powers. He doesn't trust me…

JASON: You'll never see me again. Memories are all you have left, Medea. Remember when we first met? You couldn't take your eyes off me. You cried out to heaven when I took you in the forest. Remem—

MEDEA: I remember a savage, arrogant, overweening little sailor boy whose knowledge of the universe began and ended with Greece. But he had an insatiable lust for the dark wonders of nature. The virgin Medea prayed she had at long last found a spiritual mate. So she fucked him until he became addicted to the pollen of her powers. And then I loved you beyond reason. Loving you became my life. For Jason I defied the gods, slew dragons, betrayed family; even gave to you my own eternal youth. I gave you everything you wanted, needed, asked for. *(Beat.)* Had your wife been Greek, Jason, would you have screwed her so royally?

JASON: You loved it. I was your god. The passion of my presence fired your soul. You loved my Greek rhetoric. I told you your skin was like black marble yet soft as a god's goose down. Your eyes, like radiant black pools of lust no living thing could avoid. And when you smiled the air grew musk with innocence, arousing wet and witless men and women to offer themselves in sacrifice. You were dangerously beautiful but you were no match for me. Night and day you begged Jason to caress your woolly mound of Venus; to kiss those unsuckled breasts whose wine-purple nipples tasted like dawn-sweet dew.

MEDEA: Must you dredge up memories of zestful passions spent in our youth? Are you trying to turn me on or turn yourself off?

JASON: How you loved the light of Isis,
Queen of Heaven!
You and I, Medea,
We used to ravage each other
By the light of the moon
On moist warm nights along
The banks of the Nile.
Remember?
I couldn't get enough of you,
Your moonlit blackness.

We bathed in the Nile and
Sucked pomegranates as Ra rose.
Remember, Medea, remember?

MEDEA: Still blissfully ignorant. I spoilt you. You were Medea's cute little boy, her doll husband. It's my fault, I should have raised you better. Look at you— eternally youthful, vain, full of wonder and expectation, convinced you're Zeus's gift to everything big, bad and beautiful. It's my fault. I should have taught you history, metaphysics. Perhaps I could have saved us all. Instead I went to bed with a mortal and got fucked by a metaphor.

JASON: Many women have loved Jason, and yes, men too; but none has considered it an immortal crime.

MEDEA: *(Muses.)* Medea's immortal crime is not that she loved Jason, or betrayed her country, her people, her family. Medea's unforgivable sin was to use her sacred powers to help you steal the Golden Fleece—the Cloak of Knowledge.

JASON: *(Stunned.)* The Cloak of Knowledge? The Fleece is—

MEDEA: You only saw the gold.

JASON: The Cloak of Knowledge? It's real? The Golden Fleece is the fabled Cloak of Knowledge? My god. "The one—

MEDEA: "who shoulders the Cloak will earn the right to mind the world."

JASON: No wonder they demand your head. But you don't have—

MEDEA: I have it. I have the Fleece.

JASON: You have it? But you said we lost it in Corinth.

MEDEA: I lied. I have always had it. I'm taking it back to Colchis, where it belongs.

JASON: But— why didn't you *tell* me? Why didn't you use it when we needed it? All those years of running, escaping one enemy after another, and we could have—

MEDEA: We earned our enmity, Jason. Enough is enough. This land, this is Medea's doings. I stole the light that was Africa's. If I do not return the Fleece to its proper place, Heaven and Hell will mingle on earth, and self-made demigods will lord over mortals. That's not the legacy Medea will leave her children.

JASON: The Fleece is mine, remember? You gave it to me.

MEDEA: The womb of a royal sorceress should never be opened. I loved you Jason, but you never loved me. A sorceress knows love better than most. My love protected you, sheltered your ambition, gave you a son; and when I saw that he was too African for you, I gave you one in your own image.

JASON: That's not true!

MEDEA: Don't tempt me Jason! A de-fleeced heart clothes a naked mind.

4

Power, that's all you ever wanted, Jason, and I...something higher than love. We're both ideal antagonists, Jason, but we're in two different tragedies. My drama will end when I have returned the Fleece to its proper place. Medea's epilogue will be Jason's prologue. Leave me now, Jason, I must prepare for home.

JASON: Where is it? I want the Fleece, Medea. It belongs to me.

MEDEA: Fool! It belongs to Ra! The Fleece is the sacred ram of Ra!

JASON: The sun god Ra? *(Beat.)* For god's sake, Medea! We could—

MEDEA: Forget it Jason! *(Beat.)* The Fleece is cursed. No mortal shall ever shoulder the Fleece until Medea has paid for her crime. I have agreed to make my atonement public. In exchange for this the children will become honored citizens of Colchis. It's done. Leave me now Jason. The born-again African has nothing left to give to Greece. I want to go home.

JASON: Home? To let your own people kill you? You have no home, Medea, no people. You're history, Medea, and you're Greek to the core! They'll be killing a Greek!

(Medea wags her head, No.)

MEDEA: Greek no more, Jason. You divorced Medea, remember? What's left are only memories of Medea before Jason. Colchis, where that giddy little black goddess skipped across the morning sky to greet Ra with fiery balls of laughter. How childlike her spirit. She threw half-moons like boomerangs, made jewelry out of stars and swam in sweet rain clouds. *(Beat.)* And then came Jason. So bold, so brave, so vain. I thought you were my light, my spiritual mate. By the time I realized you were just another pretty face I was the mother of your children. How appropriate for the legendary Jason and Medea to be divorced in this black/white place...this black/white time. *(Beat.)* Oh Isis, Queen of Heaven, how I long for the night divine! *(With a wave of her arm.)* Scat Day, you've overstayed your welcome!

American Medea

Silas Jones

Scene: The Mt. Vernon estate of George Washington, 1700s
> 2 Men and 1 Woman: Alexander (8), Medea's white son; Imhotep (10), Medea's black son and Helen (60s), Medea's attendant.

After many weeks at Mt. Vernon, the once loving brothers have been torn apart by the fact that they are not of the same race. Alexander has become the apple of Washington's eye whereas Imhotep has begun to fade into the large number of children in the slave quarters. Here, they passionately deny one another in the presence of their mother's attendant.

$$\bigcirc \qquad \bigcirc \qquad \bigcirc$$

(Sound of fighting kids being cheered on. Presently Alexander and Imhotep enter scuffling.)

HELEN: Children! Children!

(Offstage Children scatter and run off yelling: "It's the witch!" "Don't let her touch you!" "Run!")

IMHOTEP: Liar!

ALEXANDER: Bastard!

HELEN: *(Separating them.)* No! You mustn't fight. You're brothers! Brothers!

ALEXANDER: He's not my brother!

HELEN: Alexander! What—are you saying, Alexander?

IMHOTEP: He said we have different fathers. He called my mother a slut.

HELEN: I don't understand. You've never fought before. Who put these strange ideas into your head, Alexander?

ALEXANDER: It's as plain as the noses on our faces. Look at him; look at me? How can we possibly be brothers?

HELEN: You are the children of a royal sorceress. You're supposed to be different. You're special. You never questioned this before. This foreign land has upset your sense of harmony. Go to your mother, ask for guidance. You are her hearts, she loves you dearly.

IMHOTEP: He insulted our mother. I will not have it!

ALEXANDER: You insulted my father!

IMHOTEP: He's my father too!

ALEXANDER: He is not!

HELEN: Boys, please! You should be happy, we're finally going home. No more running and hiding from your mother's enemies.

ALEXANDER: Colchis is not my home!

IMHOTEP: You're not Greek!

ALEXANDER: Greek until I die!

HELEN: You are the sons of a Greek and an African—an African who just happens to have the power to send you back where you came from if you both don't hush. *(Beat.)* You frighten me. You are the children of a royal sorceress, joined together in a common fate. You should be proud. You're one of a kind. You either live together or—

ALEXANDER: It is not your place to lecture the son of Jason the Argonaut! You are a mere slave, a servant woman whose crude notion of Ethics was learned from the antics of an African witch!

IMHOTEP: Enough! I demand the Rite of Outcast.

HELEN: God no.

ALEXANDER: Granted!

HELEN: No boys, no no. You don't know what that means. It's different for you. For you it means…murder. Suicide. *(Backing off.)* Medea! Medea!

ALEXANDER: Helen! Stay! You are hereby designated my witness.

HELEN: No, never. I won't. This would kill your mother. Medea!

IMHOTEP: Helen, you are bound to honor the designation. I accept you as my witness.

HELEN: No, don't make me witness this. Let me call your mother. Medea! *(She tries to escape.)*

ALEXANDER: *(Declares.)* Helen of Corinth is my witness!

IMHOTEP: Helen of Corinth is my witness!

HELEN: *(Stops.)* God knows I am bound! It is the right of every kinsman. *(She turns to face them and kneels.)* Let the rite commence.

ALEXANDER: By Zeus I solemnly swear allegiance to and compliance with this Rite of Outcast. *(He uncovers his chest.)*

IMHOTEP: By Osiris I solemnly swear allegiance to and compliance with this Rite of Outcast.

(He uncovers his chest. Each places his palm over the other's naked heart.)

HELEN: Do you, Alexander, son of Jason and Medea, wish to release all blood ties to him whose heart you hold in your hand?

ALEXANDER: I do.

HELEN: Do you, Imhotep, son of Jason and Medea, wish to release all blood ties to him whose heart you hold in your hand?

IMHOTEP: I do.

HELEN: Then I, Helen of Corinth, am bound to witness. Reclaim your blood. *(Simultaneously they claw each other's heart. The blood streams down their chests.)*

ALEXANDER AND IMHOTEP: With this blood I do cast out my brother.
(They lean forward, kiss each other's heart, rear back then spit the blood into each other's face.)
HELEN: I, Helen of Corinth, bear witness to this: Alexander and Imhotep, sons of Jason and Medea, have duly exercised their right to execute the Rite of Outcast. From this day forward, under penalty of death, neither shall claim the other as brother. You are free. Go in peace. And may the gods forgive us all!

Beast on the Moon
Richard Kalinoski

Scene: Milwaukee, Wisconsin, 1921
    1 Man and 1 Woman: Aram Tomasian, 30s-40s and Seta, Armenian mail-order bride

Seta has just arrived in the United States to meet her new husband, Aram Tomasian.

○   ○   ○

MR. TOMASIAN: So. So lucky and such a great day. I have a wife…and she is in America…with me. *(Pause.)* My life can start now. My life…you know…it can start now. *(He breaks.)* My father would never imagine. Milwaukee, Wisconsin. Me, a wife.

SETA: We're both…alive.

MR. TOMASIAN: *(Abruptly.)* So, it's time for reading.

SETA: It is?

MR. TOMASIAN: *(Pleasant veneer.)* Do you have a question about everything?

SETA: It's just that I don't know very much. It's a new country.

MR. TOMASIAN: The man reads. So, I am going to read.

SETA: Umm, Mr. Tomasian, may I be permitted, excuse me, to ask why? Is that what is done with new brides who come from trains?

MR. TOMASIAN: *(A given. Inspecting her.)* My father read at all important events. At meals. At funerals. At weddings. It's in my plan.

SETA: Oh.

MR. TOMASIAN: *(Matter-of-fact.)* Nothing happens without planning.

SETA: Oh.

MR. TOMASIAN: *(Matter-of-fact.)* Why do you say 'oh'?

SETA: Mr. Tomasian, forgive me, it's just that things, everything, seems to happen all the time without planning.

MR. TOMASIAN: *(Looking for patience.)* Seta, I am going—

SETA: *(Blurting.)* Here I am in Milwaukee, no one ever planned that I was to live in America—and then the myrigs sent the wrong picture—then the big thing is I'm alive and I certainly didn't plan on being that—because everyone else is just dead—my parents—

MR. TOMASIAN: *(Patiently.)* Stop talking now, Seta.

SETA: Oh. *(She puts her head in her hands.)*

MR. TOMASIAN: What are you doing?

SETA: Nothing.

MR. TOMASIAN: This is from Timothy. Open up your ears.

(She raises her head and pulls on her ears.)

MR. TOMASIAN: *(Simply.)* "Women shall adorn themselves in modest apparel, with shamefacedness and sobriety. I suffer a woman not to teach, nor usurp authority over the man." There, now tell me, say what it means.

SETA: It means…I don't know…it means what it says.

MR. TOMASIAN: Yes, Seta. What is that?

SETA: It means…you're the man and you make the rules. I'm a girl—I mean a woman—and I'm to be quiet and serious. Except I'm not? *(He looks at her.)*

MR. TOMASIAN: What?

SETA: No…thing.

MR. TOMASIAN: Yes—something. Seta, say it.

SETA: I'm not…quiet…I have never been quiet. Mr. Tomasian, I am sorry.

MR. TOMASIAN: It will take training.

SETA: Oh.

MR. TOMASIAN: A lot of training.

SETA: Oh.

MR. TOMASIAN: So…the second reading. You like your mirror?

SETA: I love the mirror.

MR. TOMASIAN: Good. You may hold it.

(She picks up the mirror.)

MR. TOMASIAN: Hand-rubbed. American.

SETA: Yes, Mr. Tomasian.

MR. TOMASIAN: Do this. Hold the mirror out and look into it. I'll read from the Proverbs.

(Uncertain, she does this—but awkwardly.)

MR. TOMASIAN: It concerns the ideal wife. That's you. "Her husband," that's me…*(Smiling.)*

SETA: I know.

MR. TOMASIAN: "Her husband, entrusting his heart to her, has an unfailing prize."

(Mr. Tomasian smiles, and awaits a response. Seta is caught in her pose.)

MR. TOMASIAN: Well? *(He stares.)* Now tell me about Proverbs.

SETA: Well…it says that, that I am your prize. How do I be a prize?

(He regards her.)

MR. TOMASIAN: What did your parents teach you?

(She looks at him. She lets the mirror down.)

SETA: *(Quietly.)* I don't know. They loved me.

MR. TOMASIAN: Good, and what did they teach you?

SETA: They were just…just my parents. My mother sang.

MR. TOMASIAN: She sang…in a theater?

SETA: In the kitchen. *(Wistful.)* When she sang, the whole house shook and the neighbors came out into their yards. *(Glad.)*

MR. TOMASIAN: When my mother married my father she was not allowed to speak for a year. One whole year.

(Seta opens her mouth in awe. He watches her.)
MR. TOMASIAN: You don't understand. You grew up in a city. *(Smiling warmly. Speaking gently.)* This one is special and important. *(He sounds it out carefully.)* "She brings him good and not evil all the days of his life." *(He awaits her response.)* Well?
(She is in thought.)
MR. TOMASIAN: Seta?
SETA: Oh, uh, what did she do?
MR. TOMASIAN: What did who do?
SETA: Your mother, Mr. Tomasian, a whole year! She did not speak for a whole year.
MR. TOMASIAN: Haven't I asked you about Proverbs?
SETA: Yes. I'm a prize. I mean, I'm your prize.
MR. TOMASIAN: And the rest?
SETA: I'm supposed to bring good, not evil.
(He tries to discern the intention.)
MR. TOMASIAN: So, you understand.
SETA: I used to read the Bible to my father.
MR. TOMASIAN: You read the Bible? To your father? When?
SETA: Before. Before the Turk. I was a child.
MR. TOMASIAN: He didn't read it to you?
SETA: *(Giggling.)* It put him to sleep.
MR. TOMASIAN: It put him to sleep?
SETA: Oh yes, he loved it. He would start out sitting very straight. *(She postures.)* And I would read and he would go very softly...dead...uh, to the world. It was gentle music for him, I think.
MR. TOMASIAN: In my house the man reads.
(He affects a dramatic pose. She holds the mirror up.)
MR. TOMASIAN: Chapter Six, The Canticle of Canticles. "Your hair is like a flock of goats...
(She spurts.)
MR. TOMASIAN:...streaming down from Galaad."
(She giggles and then represses it.)
MR. TOMASIAN: This is the Bible!
(She quiets.)
MR. TOMASIAN: "Your teeth are like a flock of ewes which come up from the washing, all of them big with twins, none of them thin and barren."
(Her laugh explodes.)
MR. TOMASIAN: Seta, Seta, Mrs. Tomasian.
SETA: My teeth are like pregnant sheep? *(She laughs.)*
MR. TOMASIAN: These are compliments from the Bible. You laugh?
(She holds herself in.)
MR. TOMASIAN: Seta, the Bible is not funny.

SETA: Yes.

MR. TOMASIAN: The Bible speaks of beauty.

SETA: Yes, Mr. Tomasian. *(She bursts.)* Oh, oh, I'm sorry, but I started to see all the goats, a thousand goats got into my head—they were jumping around and bleating in my hair—Oh, I can't stop! *(Exploding again.)*

MR. TOMASIAN: The Bible is the breath of God.

(She finds control. He watches her, waiting for another burst. He finds the mirror and thrusts it at her.)

MR. TOMASIAN: Look at you, Mrs. Tomasian. What do you see?

(She takes the mirror, sobered.)

SETA: Me?

MR. TOMASIAN: Of course you. Who is you? Who?

SETA: I don't...I don't know.

MR. TOMASIAN: When you look, I want you to see a woman.

(She looks.)

MR. TOMASIAN: Well? Seta? *(Slowly.)* Do you see a woman?

SETA: *(Pause.)* I'm sorry. I see me.

MR. TOMASIAN: And who is that?

SETA: *(Looking.)* She's just a girl.

MR. TOMASIAN: 'She's just a girl?' 'She's just a girl?'

SETA: Thank you for this mirror, Mr. Tomasian.

(He fumes.)

SETA: I do very much want to see a woman, but I don't see one. I thank you for the mirror. And for my life.

(He paces. She gets the doll from the table.)

MR. TOMASIAN: In marriage you don't clutch dolls.

SETA: I just want to hold it. Just for now.

MR. TOMASIAN: Do you know the business of a man and a woman? *(Pause.)* Do you? *(Pause.)*

SETA: Yes. I only ask permission for the doll.

MR. TOMASIAN: *(Simply.)* No.

(She fingers the doll. He holds his hand out to take it. Very slowly, she hands it to him.)

MR. TOMASIAN: Good. I am going to wash. You say that you know about marriage. I think it's time for us to realize our marriage.

SETA: Um...I.

MR. TOMASIAN: *(Easily.)* I'll wash, I'll come back. I'll bring you in with me.

bliss
Benjamin Bettenbender

Scene: Here and now

    1 Man and 1 Woman: Jo-Lynne (30s) a woman desperate to avenge her husband's death and Chick (30s) a man who has served time for vehicular manslaughter.

A dispute between neighbors ends in bloodshed, and the grieving Jo-Lynne becomes obsessed with finding someone to kill the man who killed her husband. Here, she approaches Chick, a man she knew briefly in her past, and offers him cash to execute her husband's murderer.

○   ○   ○

JO-LYNNE: I need a favor.

(He looks at her.)

JO-LYNNE: It's more help, really. I need your help.

CHICK: Uh-huh.

JO-LYNNE: Something happened to me. To my family. And I don't know what to do about it.

CHICK: A bad thing?

JO-LYNNE: Yes. And I need some help to…I need some advice or something…Well, not advice. I know what I want to do. I just need help doing it, because—

CHICK: What happened?

JO-LYNNE: Hm?

CHICK: To your family.

JO-LYNNE: It was a few months ago. It was in all the papers and on TV and stuff.

CHICK: You were on TV?

JO-LYNNE: What happened was.

CHICK: To your family.

JO-LYNNE: Yes. And it…I mean, it was this big thing.

CHICK: Uh-huh.

JO-LYNNE: And it never got resolved. Fairly, I mean. It never got taken care of in a…just way.

CHICK: Could I ask you something?

JO-LYNNE: Sure.

CHICK: What the fuck are you talking about?

(Pause. She stares at him.)

JO-LYNNE: Did you read about the man who got killed in North Bergen last April?

CHICK: What man?

JO-LYNNE: He was in the street arguing with someone—they were having this fight, see? Shouting and cursing at each other. And this man killed him.

CHICK: Which man?

JO-LYNNE: Excuse me?

CHICK: There were two guys, who got killed? The guy who was cursing?

JO-LYNNE: Just a second. They were both cursing and… The man who was killed got killed by the guy he was fighting with.

CHICK: Shot?

JO-LYNNE: No. He hit him.

CHICK: With his hands?

JO-LYNNE: Yes.

CHICK: He killed him with…? Oh shit! Wait a second! I remember this. He had a bat, right?

JO-LYNNE: No. I just told you.

CHICK: No, the guy who got killed. He had a bat. They were arguing about something and he went in his house and got a bat. And he came out and went for the guy, and the guy caught him with an elbow shot to the nose. Killed him with a fucking elbow in like two seconds. That was all over the news, even the New York stations. He's related to you?

JO-LYNNE: My husband.

CHICK: No shit. That's hard to do, you know? Hard as hell killing someone like that. Like…Bapp! Biff! Guy's lying there like he capped him. Your husband's a seriously bad motherfucker, Jo-Lynne.

JO-LYNNE: My husband was killed.

CHICK: Oh. *(Pause.)* Oh. I thought you meant the other guy. *(Pause.)* 'Cause that is hard to do, you know? I thought about that a lot. They said he was special forces or something but still, that don't mean nothing if the guy's got a bat. You're lucky if you can maybe take it away and beat him to death with it—I mean, that's what I would try to do—but he just stepped in on him and…*(Pause. He stares at her.)* Well I guess you know all about it.

JO-LYNNE: He got off.

CHICK: Sure he did, they didn't even try it. Guy attacked him with a bat. You go after someone with a large piece of wood, you have to assume he's going to bust you back if he gets the chance.

JO-LYNNE: He got off like nothing happened. Like it was some…dispute or disagreement or something, and now it was over. Like everyone could just go back to the way they were before it happened.

CHICK: Well the other guy could, I guess.

(She stares at him, her arms held tight around herself.)

JO-LYNNE: I…

CHICK: What?

14

JO-LYNNE: I can't talk to you. I'm sorry. *(She starts to move away.)* Sorry to waste your time.

CHICK: Wait a second. I thought you wanted to talk about this.

JO-LYNNE: No.

CHICK: I thought you needed some…Whoa! Wait a second. I thought you wanted some help.

JO-LYNNE: I did, but—

CHICK: *(Blocking her path.)* So tell me.

JO-LYNNE: No.

CHICK: Come on, tell me.

JO-LYNNE: *(Moving around him.)* I made a mistake.

CHICK: What, you wanted to get the guy back or something?

(She stops; turns and looks at him.)

CHICK: You mean like that kind of help?

JO-LYNNE: Yes. *(Pause.)* I mean like that kind of help.

CHICK: Tell me.

JO-LYNNE: I want to avenge my husband.

CHICK: Avenge him how?

JO-LYNNE: You just said it.

CHICK: What did I say?

JO-LYNNE: About getting him back.

CHICK: That was a question. You want something, you say what it is.

JO-LYNNE: I want to get him back.

CHICK: Uh-huh.

JO-LYNNE: For what he did to Roberto. *(Pause.)* I want to make him pay.

CHICK: Uh-huh.

JO-LYNNE: So…I need some help.

CHICK: From me.

JO-LYNNE: I thought maybe… Yes. I thought maybe you could help me.

CHICK: In what way?

JO-LYNNE: Getting him back.

CHICK: Right, but getting him back how? You want me to key his car?

JO-LYNNE: No, I—

CHICK: You want me to doorbell-ditch him after he goes to bed.

JO-LYNNE: No. You know what I mean. You know what I'm talking about.

CHICK: Do I?

JO-LYNNE: Yes. Didn't you…I mean, weren't you away before?

CHICK: Away?

JO-LYNNE: Yeah? Weren't you?

CHICK: You mean in prison?

JO-LYNNE: Yeah.

CHICK: Sure was.

JO-LYNNE: So?

CHICK: So?

JO-LYNNE: So…I thought you could help. You know. Help.

(He stares at her a moment. He takes out another cigarette. Lights it. Stares at her.)

CHICK: Look, I'm having a little trouble here. I'm asking questions in English, and I'm getting answers in some kind of code. Not the words—the words you're saying I understand fine—but you run 'em together and they make no sense. Like gibberish. You see what I'm saying? You see the problem I'm having?

(Pause. She looks at him.)

CHICK: So what I need from you is a translation. I need one sentence that says exactly what the fuck kind of help you're standing here asking me for. You think you can do that?

(Pause.)

JO-LYNNE: I want to kill this man.

CHICK: Yeah?

JO-LYNNE: For what he did.

CHICK: And you want my help?

JO-LYNNE: Yes.

CHICK: What, you want me to hold his arms while you smack him with your husband's bat?

JO-LYNNE: No, I…*(Pause.)* I can't do it. I wasn't saying I would do it.

CHICK: You just *did* say it. You said you wanted to kill him.

JO-LYNNE: No. I meant…I want to see him die.

CHICK: You want to watch?

JO-LYNNE: No. I want him dead. I want to see to it that he dies for what he did. I want to see it done. That it *is* done, I mean. I want to see to it that it's done. You see?

(Pause. He stares at her a moment.)

CHICK: I think I kind of half-see. I mean, the part about this guy fucking you up and you wanting some payback, that I got. Hell, that's human nature. But this other part where I'm supposed to guess what it is you're asking me to do, that's another story. See, I'm almost positive what you're talking about is against the law, which makes it a violation of my parole just to have the words you're saying bouncing off my ears. So me making suggestions or whatever the fuck you're expecting, that stands to land me in a world of hurt. And all for nothing maybe. Shit, you might be wanting me to say, "No, don't do it, go talk to a priest!" but I read it wrong and tell you to go ahead and smoke him. Where does that leave me, right? So even though we're old buddies and all, I think I'm going to have to excuse myself. I think I'll go smoke inside and wait for all those cars you didn't want to block. You have yourself a real nice day.

(He turns and starts to leave.)

JO-LYNNE: I don't have anyone else.

CHICK: Pardon?

JO-LYNNE: I…I don't know anyone else. I don't have anyone else.

CHICK: What's that mean?

JO-LYNNE: To do it.

CHICK: Do what?

JO-LYNNE: What I said?

CHICK: Which is what?

JO-LYNNE: To kill him.

CHICK: Oh. You want someone to kill him *for* you. Now I understand. I understand 'cause you said it. See how that works?

JO-LYNNE: So?

CHICK: So what?

JO-LYNNE: Would you?

CHICK: Would I what?

JO-LYNNE: Do it?

(Pause.)

CHICK: Do…what?

JO-LYNNE: I'll give you twenty-three hundred dollars in cash if you'll kill the man who killed my husband. His name is Curtis Lowe. He lives on the next block over from me. He lives alone. He's home all the time. You could go any time and he'd be there. You could do it and then tell me and I could go and see—see him in his house—and you could leave and…whatever. You'd have the money. You could do whatever you want. I would just want to see it before anyone else did. It'd only take a second. *(Pause.)* Would that be OK?

CHICK: Do you know what I was in prison for, Jo-Lynne?

JO-LYNNE: Yeah. You killed someone.

CHICK: No, not what happened. The charge. Do you know what it was?

JO-LYNNE: No.

CHICK: Death by auto.

JO-LYNNE: You mean a traffic accident?

CHICK: A traffic accident that resulted in a fatality. I hit some guy while he was standing on the sidewalk. That's why I was in prison.

JO-LYNNE: Oh. But someone still died, right?

CHICK: Yeah, but it's not really the same thing. I mean, unless you want me to ring his doorbell and ask him to wait in his driveway while I run get my car, we're talking about two completely different things.

Boca
Christopher Kyle

Scene: A convenience store
   1 Man and 1 Woman: Jay (30) a man traveling to Florida in search of his parents and Linda (32) a convenience store clerk.

When Jay receives a letter from the parents he has never known, he decides to abandon his failing marriage and hitchhike to Florida. When he stops at a convenience store for some pepperoni sticks, he meets Linda, a saucy cashier who knows what she likes.

○   ○   ○

(A convenience store in Terre Haute, a few minutes later. Jay enters and begins thumbing through a magazine. Linda is behind the counter chewing gum. She watches him for a moment.)

LINDA: You gonna buy that?

JAY: Huh?

LINDA: *(As if to a child.)* Are you going to buy that?

JAY: I just picked it up.

LINDA: This ain't a library, mister.

(Pause. He puts the magazine back on the rack. She blows a bubble. He goes up to the counter and waits. Pause.)

LINDA: How may I help you?

JAY: Beef jerky.

LINDA: How many?

JAY: Two.

(She gets two out of the jar.)

JAY: No—not that. That over there.

LINDA: That's a pepperoni stick. Not beef jerky.

JAY: Whatever.

LINDA: Two?

JAY: Two.

(She lays them on the counter.)

LINDA: Is that all?

JAY: Uh…yeah.

LINDA: What about the magazine?

JAY: I don't want it.

LINDA: You got a bike?

JAY: What? A motorcycle? No.

LINDA: Then how come you're looking at the biker magazine?

JAY: It was *Sports Illustrated*.

LINDA: The hell it was. It was a biker mag. You were looking at some topless chicks, weren'tcha?

JAY: How much do I owe you?

LINDA: Let me give you a tip, my friend: we keep the good stuff under the counter. Adults only. You come in here acting like a kid—looking at biker mags—well, it makes you look awful hard up.

JAY: I'm not hard up; I'm married.

LINDA: That's the worst kind of hard up there is.

JAY: I appreciate your concern. But all I want are these two pepperoni sticks.

LINDA: You got a thing for me, don'tcha?

JAY: What?

LINDA: You come in here a lot; I've seen you. Why, this is the second time you come in here tonight.

JAY: How would you know? You weren't even here the first time I came in.

LINDA: *Ah-ha!* How would you even know that if you weren't looking for me?

JAY: Look—what's the damage for two pepperoni sticks?

LINDA: I was behind the slurpee machine, keeping spy on you. You come in, sorta nonchalant like usual, and make your way over to the magazine rack. And you keep checking for me over your shoulder, looking up at the check-out, back to the storeroom…but I was hid too good. Then you gave up and bought a couple packs of cigarettes from old Marty. You're looking to step out on your wife tonight, aren'tcha?

JAY: What's that supposed to mean?

LINDA: You're looking to cheat. But I have to tell you, I don't debase myself in that sort of manner. Usually.

JAY: My wife and I split up about five minutes ago. I left her.

LINDA: Jesus! I guess you're more serious about me than I thought.

JAY: I really just came in here for pepperoni sticks; that's all.

LINDA: Don't be so shy. You need a place to stay tonight?

JAY: *Look!* Just tell me how much I owe you and I'll be on my way.

LINDA: Dollar ninety-eight. Where're you going?

JAY: *(Giving her money.)* I'm going on a trip.

LINDA: What?

JAY: I'm on my way to meet my parents.

LINDA: Meet them where?

JAY: I mean, meet them. I've never met them before.

LINDA: How'd you manage that?

JAY: They left me at the Salvation Army when I was just a baby.

LINDA: Wow. So how'd you find them?

JAY: They sent me a letter today. I'm on my way to Florida to find out who they are.

LINDA: So how're you getting there?

JAY: Hitchhiking. I left my wife the car.

LINDA: It's a long way. There's a lot of dangerous characters out there—a fellow could get hurt.

JAY: I guess I'm looking for a little adventure.

LINDA: I might've guessed that. I could see right off you're my type.

JAY: I just want to hit the road for a while—see what I find—live from hand to mouth. I want to meet some people who'll scare the shit out of me; I want to push the boundaries of sleep deprivation. And then, when I'm at the very limit, I'll get to my parents' house and find out who I really am.

LINDA: So, hey, why don't you let me give you a lift? I get off in half an hour.

JAY: Is that your Camaro out there?

LINDA: Yeah.

JAY: Nice car.

LINDA: Thanks.

JAY: Okay.

LINDA: Hi. My name is Linda.

JAY: Hi. I'm Jay.

By The Sea: Dusk

Terrence McNally

Scene: The beach at dusk
    1 Man and 2 Women: Willy, jogger at beach; Dana, jogger at beach; and Marsha, swimmer at beach.

Dana, Willy and Marsha run into each other at the beach at dusk.

○   ○   ○

DANA: Hi.

MARSHA: Don't mind me.

DANA: I beg your pardon?

MARSHA: I said, don't mind me.

DANA: I wasn't.

MARSHA: "So why does she have to come right over to where I am when she has the whole goddamn beach to herself?" Go on, admit it. I know that's what your were thinking.

DANA: Well.

MARSHA: I don't blame you. If I were you, I'd want to kill me. When I think I have the whole beach to myself and someone comes within even a hundred yards of me I want to murder them. Since we can't do that, let's hear it for civilization, rah rah rah, sis boom bah! I fix them with my deadliest glare instead. You know that expression: if looks could kill? Mine do. They drop like flies. Every time they look over at me they get this pair of really deadly eyes just glaring at them.

(Willy returns from jogging.)

MARSHA: This is just what I was talking about. Just dare look over here, buster, just dare. I'll give you such a look, you won't know what hit you.

WILLY: Hi, there, gorgeous.

MARSHA AND DANA: Hi.

MARSHA: I'm sorry, I thought you were talking to me.

DANA: *(Overlapping.)* Excuse me, I thought you were.

(Willy quickly strips and runs into the ocean.)

DANA: You could move.

MARSHA: Of course, I could move, but why should I have to move? I was here first. Am I right?

DANA: I suppose.

MARSHA: Of course in this case, you think you were here first. Wrong. I was here before you. Of course millions of people were here before me but this isn't about them. This is about us. So here's the story. I lost my car keys right about where you are.

DANA: That's terrible.

MARSHA: I don't want your pity.

DANA: I wouldn't exactly call it pity. It was more like empathy.

(Willy returns from swimming.)

WILLY: I'm not going to fight that undertow. I don't recommend that you do either.

MARSHA: Some people just won't take "no" for an answer!

WILLY: This is my favorite time of day here. The beach is usually empty. You have it pretty much to yourself. And if you do run into someone, they're usually pretty interesting. At least they're more interested in their souls than in their suntans. This is my favorite time of year here, too. The water's still warm enough to swim. The really gross people have gone back to their rabbit warrens in the teeming cities and/or stifling hamlets of this sadly/gently, yet somehow-still-great declining nation of ours and only we, the semi-gross, for no one completely escapes the blight, only we three remain to bask in the last warm days of summer when the sunsets are like a golden blanket you can wrap around you.

MARSHA: That was very poetic.

WILLY: Thank you. I try.

MARSHA: It was. It was.

WILLY: Where was I?

MARSHA: I'm sorry, I didn't mean to interrupt.

DANA: The beach at sunset.

WILLY: Thank you. Some of the most meaningful relationships in my life have begun on the beach at sunset. At high noon on the strand, all you meet are people with a death wish. I'm talking about skin cancer. I learned my lesson the hard way. My doctor said, "Keep it up, Willy, and I'm going to be a rich man cutting the skin cancers out of you. Just keep it up. Me and my scalpels'll be waiting for you."

MARSHA AND DANA: *(Wincing.)* Oooo!

WILLY: He didn't say that really. You have to exaggerate in life or people don't get the point you're making. It's not enough to say "I love you" anymore. You have to say it more like ten million times. I love you, I love you, I love you, I love you, I love you, I love you. Eventually, if you're lucky, and not hoarse or bored to death from saying it so much, they get it. "I get it! He loves me!" Of course by that time, you've probably moved on and are loving somebody else.

MARSHA: That is so, so sad.

DANA: That is so true.

WILLY: Where was I?

DANA: Love.

MARSHA: The impossibility of love.

WILLY: Skin cancer. My point is this: the sun, the source of life, is a killer. That's called a paradox. You don't look like ladies I have to explain what a paradox is to, so I won't. But I don't blush to tell you I didn't know one from a handsaw until Dr. Landeau started talking to me about those skin cancers unless I changed my wicked, wicked ways. I was a sun worshipper. I used to think a great tan was one of the three meanings of life. Don't ask me what the other two were. Boy, did I have my head up my ass! *Sur la plage* is no longer a safe place to be except at night. Or now. Now is safe.

MARSHA: Now is beautiful. Such delicate colors. That pale moon already shimmering on the cusp of a lilac/lavender horizon.

WILLY: Way to go, babe, way to go! You've got a touch of the poet yourself.

MARSHA: Don't tell Dr. Gluck.

WILLY: I hope neither of you object to being called "babe."

DANA: I don't know about her but I do.

WILLY: You mustn't take it personally. It's strictly generic. I grew up on Sonny and Cher.

DANA: Well maybe it's time you outgrew them. Cher did.

MARSHA: That wasn't called for.

WILLY: Thank you. Your friend.

MARSHA: She's not my friend.

DANA: Please don't refer to me in the third person like that. It's very dismissive, thank you.

WILLY: Do you have a name?

DANA: Of course I have a name. Everyone has a name.

WILLY: What is it? I'd like to use it.

DANA: Never mind.

WILLY: That female of the species I mistakenly identified you as being with has a real bug up her ass.

MARSHA: I guess she does.

DANA: Look who's talking! She was the one making faces. And I don't have a bug up my ass. I resent you saying that. How do you know what I have up my ass? I was fine until she showed up.

MARSHA: Hi. I'm Marsha.

WILLY: I'm Willy.

DANA: All right. My name is Dana. Are you satisfied?

WILLY: So who's this Dr. Gluck?

MARSHA: My analyst.

WILLY: I figured.

DANA: I don't feel comfortable giving you my last name, okay?

WILLY: Gluck means happy in German. Hell of a name for a therapist. You have wonderful breasts.

MARSHA: Thank you.

WILLY: Okay, Donna, your turn now. What can I do for you?

DANA: It's Dana. You can't do anything for me.

Cloud Tectonics

José Rivera

Scene: Present, Los Angeles, night
    1 Man and 1 Woman: Celestina Del Sol (20s) and Aníbal De La Luna (30s).

Aníbal sees pregnant Celestina standing at a bus stop in a driving rain. He stops his car and takes her in.

○   ○   ○

CELESTINA: *(Shivering.)* Thank you so much for this.

ANÍBAL: Jesus, you're soaked. There's a jacket in the back seat.

CELESTINA: *(Putting on jacket.)* Thank you.

(Short beat.)

ANÍBAL: I can't believe anyone's out in that deluge. They're calling it the storm of the century.

CELESTINA: Where am I?

ANÍBAL: Los Angeles.

CELESTINA: *(Troubled.)* Los Angeles?

ANÍBAL: Corner of Virgil and Santa Monica.

CELESTINA: *(Means nothing to her.)* Oh.

(Celestina says no more. She just rubs her pregnant stomach and stares ahead. Her silence makes Aníbal a little nervous.)

ANÍBAL: Can you believe this rain for L.A.? *Coño!* Raging floods on Fairfax…bodies floating down the L.A. River…LAX closed…if the Big One came right now, forget it, half this city would die. But that's L.A. for you: disasters just waiting to happen.

(Aníbal laughs. No response from Celestina.)

ANÍBAL: I lived in New York. Lived in every borough except Staten Island. And Brooklyn. And Queens. And the thing is, New York kills its people one-by-one, you know? A gun here, a knife there, hand-to-hand combat at the ATM, little countable deaths. But this? This L.A. thing? *Mass* death, *mass* destruction. One freak flood at the wrong time of year and hundreds die…the atmosphere sags from its own toxic heaviness and thousands perish…the Big One is finally born, eats a hundred thousand souls for *breakfast.* And I'm not even talking fire season!

(Celestina looks at Aníbal for the first time.)

CELESTINA: Why don't you go back to New York?

ANÍBAL: Are you kidding? I love it here. I have a house here. I have gorgeous fucking incredible-looking women falling outta the sky here! *Coño,* I've made a commitment to that!

(No response from Celestina. She eats a cracker quietly, her mind far away. Anibal looks at her a long moment.)

ANÍBAL: You all right?

CELESTINA: The trucker that dropped me off kept touching my knees and I screamed.

ANÍBAL: How long were you out there?

(Beat.)

CELESTINA: I don't know.

ANÍBAL: You don't know?

(Beat.)

CELESTINA: I don't have a watch…I don't keep a watch…I don't keep "time"…"Time" and I don't hang out together!

ANÍBAL: *(Not understanding.)* Oh. Where can I take you?

CELESTINA: I don't know. Away from the rain?

ANÍBAL: Tough luck; it's everywhere. Where were you hitching to?

CELESTINA: Nowhere. I'm not going anywhere. I don't know where I'm going, I'm sorry.

ANÍBAL: You're just out there hitching? In a hurricane? Pregnant? For fun?

CELESTINA: Are you going to ask me a lot of questions?

ANÍBAL: Why don't I take you to a hospital? Get someone to check out your baby.

CELESTINA: No! No! Don't do that! I don't want doctors asking me a lot of questions!

ANÍBAL: Maybe the police could…

CELESTINA: No police! Please! No police! I don't want to go to the police!

ANÍBAL: No friends or family in L.A.?

CELESTINA: No one. I have no one. You're the only one I know!

ANÍBAL: *(Choosing to ignore that.)* Well, you're in my car, I gotta take you somewhere…

CELESTINA: Take me to this baby's father. I'm looking for this baby's father. His name is Rodrigo Cruz. Do you know him? He's a very handsome and dishonest man.

ANÍBAL: No, I don't think I…

CELESTINA: Nobody knows him. I ask everybody. That trucker took me to every state looking for Rodrigo Cruz!

ANÍBAL:…I'm sorry…

CELESTINA: I started my journey on Montauk Point: A room in a house, very small, my Papi sailed boats for tourists, it was some distance back—but I—I lost all track of "time"—I hate to use that word—"time"—but it's the only word I have, isn't it?

ANÍBAL: *Coño,* I'm not following this…

CELESTINA: I can give you *details* of Rodrigo Cruz. He worked for Papi repairing the boat. His eyes were ocean-green. His back was wrinkled. But I can't tell you *when* he was like that, okay? He might have *changed,* you see? I can't tell you his *age.* Do you know how hard it is to find someone when you can't tell anyone their age?

ANÍBAL: Well, it's not a problem I ever…

CELESTINA: All this traveling has been a blur! It's a huge country! I never should have left my house in Montauk! I was safe in my house! Papi and Mami had it all worked out for me! They took away all the clocks!

ANÍBAL: *(Completely lost.)* The clocks?

CELESTINA: But I was sleeping when that gorgeous son-of-a-bitch Rodrigo Cruz came into my room! He knocked me up! He left! Now look at me! I'm starving and lost and sick of these soggy *fucking* crackers…and I'm just so tired of being *pregnant!*

ANÍBAL: *(Worried.)* Take it easy…

CELESTINA: You can let me out right here, I'm sorry!

ANÍBAL: But we haven't moved. Light's still red.

CELESTINA: Oh. Right. *(Celestina cries and stuffs her mouth with crackers.)*

ANÍBAL: You all right?

CELESTINA: Please, I don't want to bother you anymore.

ANÍBAL: I don't want you sleeping outside. Not with a baby coming.

CELESTINA: I've done it before!

(The relentless rain slaps the car as Aníbal contemplates his options.)

ANÍBAL: *Coño,* okay, listen: if you promise me you're not an ax-murderer…I promise you *I'm* not an ax-murderer too, okay? You can stay in my house tonight, okay? Just tonight, okay? I'm right up here in Echo Park, okay?

CELESTINA: I can? I can't.

ANÍBAL: I promise not to touch your knees, okay?

(Celestina looks at Aníbal.)

CELESTINA: What's your name?

ANÍBAL: Oh I'm sorry. Aníbal de la Luna. Nice to meet you.

CELESTINA: I'm Celestina del Sol.

(She reaches out her hand. Aníbal and Celestina shake hands. She smiles.)

CELESTINA: Okay. Let's go to your place.

(The light turns green. The lights go down on Aníbal and Celestina.)

Dance With Me

Jean Reynolds

Scene: Upstate New York, 1950s
    1 Man and 2 Women: Ray (40s); Ruth (30-40) his wife and Grace (30-40) his mistress.

Ray has promised to leave Ruth for Grace, but so far has been unable to do so. In order to appease Grace, Ray has given her a job in his medical office so that they may spend more time together. Canny Ruth immediately perceives that something has changed in her husband's demeanor and invites Grace to tea so that she may get a better look at the woman who seems to be changing her life. When the rivals finally meet they are instantly attracted to one another and a tentative friendship begins. Here, all three are gathered at Ray and Ruth's for dinner. During cocktails, Ruth tries to gently uncover the truth about Ray and Grace by asking her new friend pointed questions about the boyfriend she claims to be in love with.

O   O   O

GRACE: I'll tell you about my boyfriend.

RAY: You don't have to.

GRACE: I want to. *(Pause.)* My boyfriend loves two women.

RUTH: *(To Ray.)* What do you think of that?

RAY: Two women?

RUTH: Grace's boyfriend loves two women. What do you think of that? A theoretical question.

RAY: What do I think, theoretically, of Grace's boyfriend loving two women?

RUTH: What do you think?

RAY: It's possible.

RUTH: To love two women?

RAY: Yes.

GRACE: Equally?

RAY: Equally.

RUTH: Exactly the same?

RAY: I didn't say exactly the same. I said equally.

GRACE: It happens, I suppose.

RAY: You can't predict it but—

RUTH: It happens.

GRACE: Love is limitless.

RAY: It's not as though there's a certain amount and it gets used up.

GRACE: It's inexhaustible.

RUTH: Enough for everybody.

28

RAY: Enough to go around. More gin?

GRACE: Please.

RUTH: Someone suffers.

RAY: Someone doesn't have to.

RUTH: But someone does.

RAY: It's between Grace and her boyfriend.

RUTH: Leave him.

GRACE: Leave him?

RUTH: That's my advice. Leave him.

RAY: Leave him?

RUTH: He's not going to abandon his wife.

RAY: He might. I'm not saying he would. He probably wouldn't. I don't know.

RUTH: What should she do?

RAY: Who?

RUTH: His wife.

RAY: I thought you meant Grace.

RUTH: I feel sorry for his wife.

GRACE: I'm the one making sacrifices.

RUTH: We all make sacrifices.

GRACE: I'm the one alone most of the time. I'm the one with the half-life, waiting for calls, sneaking around, hoping.

RUTH: She probably loves him.

GRACE: Who?

RUTH: His wife.

GRACE: I thought you meant me.

RAY: You'd have left him by now if you didn't love him.

RUTH: What about his wife?

RAY: What about his wife?

RUTH: What if she left him?

RAY: She wouldn't.

RUTH: She might.

GRACE: You're assuming she knows. She may know. Or she may not.

RAY: She'd have left if she wanted to.

RUTH: Something keeps his wife from leaving. Habit. Or need. Or comfort. Or she has nowhere to go. Or...or it's love.

GRACE: Does she know?

RUTH: His wife?

GRACE: Does she?

RUTH: She knows him.

GRACE: If she knew, what would she do?

RUTH: Kill him.

RAY: Kill him?

RUTH: She ought to.

RAY: Kill him?

RUTH: It's quite natural.

GRACE: It's extreme.

RAY: He deserves to be killed, that's true. But he's only a man trying to live his life the best way he can. I'm not making excuses. Well, yes, I am. He's only a man who—

RUTH: You amuse me.

RAY: Why?

RUTH: Because you do.

RAY: You amuse me.

RUTH: Why?

RAY: Because you do.

GRACE: You both amuse me.

RUTH: His wife knows.

RAY: What makes you say that?

RUTH: A hunch.

RAY: I feel sorry for him.

GRACE: Why?

RUTH: *(To Ray.)* What if Grace moved in with them?

GRACE: What?!

RAY: Ruth!

GRACE: That would be something, wouldn't it?

RAY: *(To Ruth.)* You're embarrassing Grace.

RUTH: Grace is friends with his wife.

GRACE: Close friends.

RUTH: If Grace moved in with them, his wife would have someone to…to talk to. Someone to keep her company when he goes away. *(To Grace.)* He travels.

GRACE: Yes.

RUTH: Plenty of room in the house. *(To Grace.)* It's a big house.

GRACE: Yes.

RUTH: What if Grace moved in with them?

RAY: Ridiculous. Absurd. Impossible. Unthinkable. Completely unthinkable. Totally and completely unthinkable. Would his wife agree?

RUTH: Yes! What an idea. His wife suggests it.

GRACE: What an idea.

RUTH: Let's say the arrangement falls into place and Grace is living with them. *(To Ray.)* Is that what he wants?

RAY: It's…it's unusual…intriguing.

GRACE: There's one thing, though.

RAY: What?

GRACE: Well, I mean, well, all right, maybe his wife knows about…knows… well, she knows. Maybe she does. Let's say she does and seems to—

RUTH: To accept it?

GRACE: To accept it, yes. To let it be…for various reasons, for her reasons, and well, what I want to know is what happens when he finds out—

RAY: Finds out what?

GRACE: He thinks of the arrangement as his. His double marriage.

RUTH: His wives?

GRACE: At first it doesn't occur to him.

RAY: What doesn't occur to him?

GRACE: As they sit on the porch and read the evening paper and sip their gin and talk. As they listen to the frogs and crickets, the crunch of gravel as cars pass by. The whistle of the night train. It doesn't occur to him.

RAY: What?

GRACE: When he gets up from his wife's bed and quietly searches for his slippers.

RUTH: Brown leather slippers.

GRACE: When he tiptoes across the room—

RUTH: Trying not to wake his wife.

GRACE: Into the hall.

RUTH: Careful of creaking floorboards.

GRACE: Down the passage to my room. He doesn't realize that his wife and I…his wife and I…He doesn't realize.

RAY: Realize what?

GRACE: One night he arrives home early.

RUTH: To enjoy his double marriage.

GRACE: He pushes open the front door. Where are they? He hears something. Dance music. He follows the music to its source.

RUTH: *(To Ray, indicating glass.)* Pour a little more gin in here, will you?

RAY: Certainly. *(He does.)*

GRACE: A white curtain at the window, translucent, the garden beyond, late afternoon, the buzz and hum of nature, a breeze from the open window stirs the perfumes, blending them, his wife's and mine. He sees us, and knows.

RAY: What if he already knows?

Dates and Nuts

Gary Lennon

Scene: New York City
    1 Man and 1 Woman: Donald (30s) a Regular Joe who tries too hard and Eve (30s) very
    excitable, hyper, tough edge, wild.

The bombastic Eve has just been stood up at a bar and is none too pleased about it. As she fumes to herself about the ruined evening, she is suddenly accosted by the incredibly pushy Donald.

○   ○   ○

DONALD: Hi! How are you doing?

(No answer.)

DONALD: Can I buy you a drink? My name is Donald.

EVE: I'm an alcoholic, Donald! I'm allergic to alcohol. The last time I drank I shot a man who looked just like you. May I have another vodka tonic please?

DONALD: That was a joke, right? That's funny…I guess you don't want a drink then?

EVE: Bingo!

DONALD: I just came from having the best dinner I ever had in my life. I cooked it myself. I'm a great cook. I like to cook.

EVE: Oh, that's cute. You like to cook? You like to wear dresses too? Are you a "G"?!

DONALD: What? How about you?

(No answer.)

DONALD: Do you like to cook? Huh? Huh?

EVE: I'm not deaf. I'm ignoring you! *(Quietly.)* I'm not interested in you. OK?

DONALD: What? You're shy, huh? You find it hard talking to people. You have to become more outgoing like me…I have a few cookbooks. I love to cook. I could teach you.

EVE: Fairies like to cook. Are you a fairy? You look like an old gladiola face. Mums are dangling from your nose.

DONALD: What?

EVE: Are you a Mary, a "G," a homosexual?

DONALD: What?

EVE: I think you are a big "G." All of you are! You have tulips coming out of your nose. You can't fool me. You're in full bloom.

DONALD: What are you talking about?

EVE: Leave me alone.

DONALD: I don't understand what you just said.

EVE: That's right. Play dumb. Be a Mary!

(Pause. Donald takes a different tack.)

DONALD: Where are you from?

EVE: Excuse me, I'm sorry. I know you're trying to be charming, but I forgot your name. Can I just call you asshole?

DONALD: My name is Donald.

EVE: Donald, asshole, you repel me. Go away.

DONALD: You don't like men.

EVE: What gives you that idea?

DONALD: Cause you're bagging me.

EVE: Nooo.

DONALD: See, I wasn't sure. What's your favorite color? Did you know that most people say blue?

EVE: You watch too many game shows, Donald.

DONALD: No, I don't. I don't even have a TV. You didn't tell me where you're from.

EVE: I'm from planet fucking Pluto, and that's quite a trip, and I gotta get back, so I'm gonna get going. *(She begins to leave and stops.)* No, I'm waiting for my friend. Would you please leave me alone? Give me my space.

DONALD: First, tell me where you're from.

EVE: You don't give up, do you? Please! If I tell you, will you avoid me at all costs?

(He doesn't respond.)

EVE: I'm from a far, far away place called Brooklyn.

DONALD: I used to be a selfish lover. I used to always have to be on top.

EVE: I'm charmed. Do you discuss this with everyone?

DONALD: No, but I have a feeling you understand. But I'm not like that any more… I mean I'm working on it. I used to have a big list of sexual things I did and things that I didn't do, but I'm sort of relaxing on them now. You see, I used to only want to get off, you know, satisfy myself, and that's it, but I'm starting to like, you know, want to be friends with the girls that I pork. You know, sort of talk to them and stuff. You know what I mean.

EVE: Pork. Charming… I'm sure they're pleased.

DONALD: *(Whispers.)* Sometimes I like it rough…

EVE: Don't even think about it, OK?

DONALD: You look like you like it rough.

33

EVE: Why don't I tie you up to the bar and beat the shit out of you right here so you can get on with the rest of your life and leave me alone, OK?

DONALD: I don't like crowds, but let's discuss it.

EVE: Help! You need help!

DONALD: Oh, and what do you do?

EVE: What, are you writing a book?

DONALD: No! I just like talking to people, it's my thing—

EVE: I work for the Humane Society. I'm an animal rights activist. Right now I'm involved with the African elephant. Now would you please leave me alone.

DONALD: I hope not too involved. Ha, ha, ha.

EVE: I take it very seriously. Jerk!! Animals are a serious thing.

DONALD: I'm a lawyer. Are you a dyke?

EVE: If it's easier for your ego, since I'm rejecting you, to rationalize that I'm a lesbian, go ahead and believe it. I love women.

DONALD: You don't like me, is that what you're saying? You're not attracted to me. I'm not good enough for you, is that it? Something wrong with me!

EVE: Please! Look, I don't have the time to give free self-esteem courses, OK?

DONALD: You are a bitch!

EVE: You have such a way with words.

DONALD: You are a real bitch.

EVE: And so is your Aunt Lulu!

DONALD: You're in a good mood.

EVE: What?

DONALD: You better put yourself on the endangered species list. You are a pig!

EVE: Yes, I'm a pig! *And I love it!* Being a pig is one of my favorite things. I thank God every day that I'm a pig! *Leave!* You repulse me.

DONALD: You're a dyke.

EVE: Who are you?! What am I doing here talking to you! Who are you to be prejudiced? You're a bum. Get away from me. You repulse me. Everything you stand for disgusts me!! You disgust me. Your face disgusts me. Your voice disgusts me!! You violate my sense of aestheticism. You are ugly to me, understand? *Ugly!* Everything about you is alien to my being! You make me want to throw up! Puke! Your maleness is detestable. You make my skin crawl! I am physically revolted by you! I cringe when I see you. I hate your mother for having you. I loathe your teeth. I choose not to receive you in any way, shape or form! I hate your father and his friends, and your shoes smell. I do not like you. Go away!! I reject you! You are a banana!

DONALD: *(Laughing.)* Go save an elephant, will ya? Look, if I'm not going to fuck you, let's try and be friends, OK?

EVE: Haven't you heard anything I said? I despise you!

DONALD: You're just saying that.

EVE: No, I'm not. Believe me, I mean it.

DONALD: I'm tired of talking to these stupid girls. At least you have some spunk. You can hold a conversation.

EVE: I don't believe this.

DONALD: I mean after I screw them, I wanna be able to talk to them, you know what I'm saying?

EVE: I'm afraid so.

DONALD: I can talk to you! I dig you.

EVE: You are a slime, can you not see that? An animal male slime.

DONALD: *(Laughs.)* What, you want to talk about the elephants again?

EVE: I do not appreciate your joking! These African elephants are dying. They are becoming extinct. You…it's not funny. Get political!

DONALD: Look, I was just making conversation.

EVE: Conversation! Conversation! Stop talking and do something for Christ's sake. Stop thinking with your penis. I see the way you're looking at me! As you stand there salivating over my legs, some poacher in Africa is killing an elephant to make a fucking bracelet. He is ripping the front of his face off to get ivory! How would you like someone to rip the front of your face off? It's sick. It's wrong, can't you see that? It's all about money. You are a hormone!

DONALD: Hey, this is a bar, a party, a free country, all right? I just wanted…

EVE: Want! Want! Want! Want! Want! Want!

DONALD: What the fuck…

EVE: I wanted my life to be mystical, really Japanese, but it just didn't turn out that way! Did it? Nooo! Waiting for men to make me happy! No more!

DONALD: You need to get laid, you pent up wench! It's people like you that make me thank God every time I take care of it myself!

EVE: Don't fuck with me, Cinderella!!

Drive Like Jackson Pollock
Steven Tanenbaum

Scene: Here and now
  1 Man and 1 Woman: Brando (20-30) a man disabled in a car crash and hunted by never-ending physical and emotional pain and Celina (20-30) the cigar-smoking Latina hedonist who loves him.

Here, Brando, a jazz lover, meets Celina for the first time.

○　　　○　　　○

CELINA: What are those? *(She points to the mini CDs Brando is carrying with him.)*

BRANDO: *(Brando takes off the headset to his Walkman and holds up one of the mini CDs.)* These? Mini CDs.

CELINA: They're so cute.

BRANDO: Just another format that'll be obsolete tomorrow.

CELINA: What are you listening to?

BRANDO: Coltrane.

CELINA: What kind of music is that?

BRANDO: For me, religious.

CELINA: Can I hear?

(He hands her the earphones. Listens for a moment before handing them back.)

CELINA: Sounds like jazz.

BRANDO: Are you into jazz?

CELINA: I like that guy—Thelonious Monk.

BRANDO: You like Monk?

CELINA: My favorite song is *'Round Midnight.*

BRANDO: You like Monk?

CELINA: Do you like him?

BRANDO: Do I like Monk. Man. Let's put it this way: I once made a pact with myself that if I ever met a girl who liked Monk I'd have to marry her on the spot.

CELINA: Just because she liked Monk?

BRANDO: See, jazz fans are already an endangered species. And when I say fan, I'm not talking about that Bill Clinton: "Kenny G. is my favorite saxophonist" crap that they play when you're getting teeth drilled. I'm talking about the real deal—Bird, Diz, Powell and Monk. That's my glass slipper if you can swing to it. But so far my bop Cinderella has eluded me. I mean— you really like Monk?

CELINA: *(Nods.)* You'd really marry her on the spot?

BRANDO: Have to.

CELINA: Where's the ring?

BRANDO: In the vault.

CELINA: "In the vault." I like the sound of that.

BRANDO: Tell me, what do you like best?

CELINA: Nothing less than 9 carats.

BRANDO: No, I mean about Monk.

CELINA: His hat. What do you call them?

BRANDO: Pork Pie. I can't believe you even know what type of hat he wore.

CELINA: When can I see the ring?

BRANDO: Whenever you want. Do you want to listen to '*Round Midnight* now. I've got it with me…*(He rummages around in his CD case.)* I could swear I brought it…

CELINA: You looking for this? *(Holds up the Monk mini CD.)* You dropped it back there.

BRANDO: Does this mean you don't like Monk?

CELINA: Does this mean I don't get the ring?

Fortune's Fools
Frederick Stroppel

Scene: New York City

    2 Men and 2 Women: Chuck and Gail, a couple about to be married and their respective best friends, Jay and Bonnie.

Chuck and Gail have introduced Jay and Bonnie, thinking that they'd make a good couple. Unfortunately, carnivorous Jay and vegetarian Bonnie have nothing in common and form an instant dislike of one another. Bonnie, who is an actress, is currently performing in a version of The Taming of the Shrew *in which the genders of Kate and Petruccio have been reversed. Chuck and Gail drag Jay to a performance, and after the show Bonnie's and Jay's fireworks continue. (It is important to note that Bonnie and Jay wind up madly in love.)*

(Chuck, Gail, and Jay exit the theater. Their faces clearly express how bad it was. They pause to take a collective deep breath.)

CHUCK: So that was supposed to be a comedy?

GAIL: *(Striving to be upbeat.)* She really commands the stage, doesn't she? I didn't notice one mistake.

CHUCK: But I don't get it. Why was his name Kate?

(Bonnie comes out, still half in costume.)

BONNIE: Hey!

GAIL: Here she is! *(Bestowing kisses on Bonnie.)* That was wonderful!

CHUCK: Great. Great.

BONNIE: Thank you...

GAIL: You were so *funny.* I got that 'chattels' line.

BONNIE: *(Notices the conspicuously silent Jay.)* Jay, isn't it? You didn't have to come.

JAY: But I'm glad I did.

BONNIE: I hope you enjoyed it. It wasn't *Miss Saigon,* of course...

JAY: No, *Miss Saigon* had some laughs.

GAIL: *(Trying to avoid hostilities.)* So are we going someplace for a bite to eat? We have more wedding news.

CHUCK: What I don't get, though, is why the guy's name is Kate. I've been to Italy a couple of times, and nobody's named Kate.

GAIL: It's poetic license, dope.

BONNIE: We tried to preserve the integrity of the language wherever possible.

JAY: It would have been nice if you preserved the integrity of the ideas, too.

BONNIE: The ideas are archaic. After all, Shakespeare was strait-jacketed by the conventions of a repressed society. He had to disguise his real intentions.

JAY: Oh, give me a break. If he came right out and said that women should be subservient to men, then that's what he meant. This is not a guy who had difficulty expressing himself.

BONNIE: That's just an uninformed surface reading. If you examine the subtext...

JAY: *(In nursery singsong.)* Shakespeare was a sexist, Shakespeare was a sexist...

BONNIE: What could you possibly know about Shakespeare? What, do you have a Classics Illustrated disk in your computer?

JAY: I know the difference between Masterpiece Theater and Masturbation Theater.

BONNIE: I'm sure you speak from firsthand experience. Or maybe you're just threatened by the sight of a woman assuming the male's traditional role of swaggering dominance.

JAY: I'm threatened by the tidal wave of politically correct bullshit that's overflowing this country like a sewage backup...

BONNIE: Hey, women have the ascendant role in our society. If you can't deal with that, then grow yourself a beard and move to Iran.

JAY: Why don't you?

BONNIE: Why don't *you?*

CHUCK: Guys, guys...

(Jay and Bonnie back off.)

JAY: *(Shrugs.)* Just stating my opinion.

BONNIE: It's a free country. Excuse me, I have to change.

(Bonnie heads upstage to change; Gail follows to give her a hand.)

CHUCK: You know, a simple "congratulations" would have been enough.

JAY: I can't help it. She's such an easy target. I really nailed her with that "Masterpiece Theater" line.

CHUCK: She got you back with the "hand" bit.

JAY: Oh, please. She never touched me.

CHUCK: Man, this is gonna be a long night.

(Over to Gail and Bonnie.)

GAIL: Why do you have to keep getting the better of him?

BONNIE: Because it's fun. He invites derision—what can I say?

GAIL: Can't you try to behave yourself, for my sake?

BONNIE: I told you not to bring him.

(Back to Jay and Chuck.)

JAY: I told you to keep her away from me.

CHUCK: I'm not asking you to sleep with her. Just don't antagonize her. As a favor to me.

JAY: You want me to be nice? All right. I'll be a saint. But if she says one word...

(Bonnie and Gail return.)

GAIL: Are we ready?

(Bonnie and Jay pointedly avoid looking at each other, and stand as far apart as possible. They head out of the theater, and stand in the street.)

CHUCK: So where do you wanna eat? I think I saw a pasta place around the corner...

GAIL: Oh, we finally found a band. Johnny A. and the Sophisticatos. They're really good.

CHUCK: They're really expensive.

JAY: You should have gotten a DJ. They cost half the price, and they can play anything you want.

(Bonnie mutters under her breath.)

JAY: Excuse me?

BONNIE: No, nothing.

GAIL: This band is versatile. They do rock and pop, and the old stuff, too—you know, Glenn Miller and show tunes...

CHUCK: *(Ready to move on.)* It's cold out here, isn't it?

BONNIE: Well, I'm disappointed. I was hoping you'd go with a string quartet.

(Jay suppresses a laugh.)

BONNIE: Did you have something to say?

JAY: No that would be lovely. Lovely.

BONNIE: It seems to me a touch of elegance might offset some of the more common elements. Like "the bride cuts the cake," or throwing the bouquet...

GAIL: I kinda like that stuff. *(To Chuck.)* Don't you?

JAY: Maybe you should have the groom throw the bouquet. Or the bride throw the groom.

BONNIE: It's just corny and outdated, that's all I'm saying.

JAY: You might as well say that marriage is outdated.

BONNIE: Maybe it is. Maybe the selling and bartering of women for economic or sexual reasons is an idea whose time has come and gone.

JAY: *(Scoffs.)* Who invented marriage in the first place? It wasn't a man, I can tell you that.

BONNIE: Oh, sure, women just couldn't wait to surrender their individuality and their dreams to the first ape who got up off his knuckles and combed his eyebrows.

JAY: I don't think men were going around saying, "Here, take my money, take my freedom, take my soul, please!"

BONNIE: Who wrote every single misogynistic Judeo-Christian law regarding the proper role of the submissive wife? Who devised the chastity belt, and the corset, and the Rule of Thumb?

JAY: Who ate the apple?

(Bonnie is speechless with disbelief.)

JAY: Aha. From whence all our miseries derive.

CHUCK: Is anybody else cold? I'm freezing.

BONNIE: You know, I misjudged you, Jay. At first I thought you were just an ordinary middle-class anti-intellectual boor. But now I can see, you're really a classic American primitive. A total anachronism.

JAY: And you're a pretentious snob.

BONNIE: An ignorant yahoo.

JAY: An obnoxious airhead.

BONNIE: A loser.

JAY: A nitwit.

BONNIE: No, that's you.

JAY: No, that's *you*.

(Bonnie and Jay walk off, continuing their discussion. Chuck and Gail watch with dismay.)

GAIL: *(Stubbornly optimistic.)* There's a chemistry there. I know it.

Half-Court
Brian Silberman

Scene: Here and now
    1 Man and 1 Woman: David (30s) and Susan, two singles searching for love.

Susan and David have just participated in a sexual encounter that was far from satisfactory. Here, they discuss the damage.

O   O   O

(David and Susan lie side by side, in bed. Their clothes are strewn around the room. There is a slight pause.)

DAVID: I'm sorry.

SUSAN: Forget it.

DAVID: No really. That usually doesn't happen. Usually I have more control.

SUSAN: It's all right.

DAVID: Look…give me a few minutes and we can—

SUSAN: Maybe we should just forget it.

DAVID: No, no.

SUSAN: I wasn't sure this was such a great idea to begin with.

DAVID: Susan.

SUSAN: Maybe we should just treat this as a sign, okay?

DAVID: Why would you say that? We were doing fine. I just…just give me a couple of minutes and we can—

SUSAN: *(Rising and beginning to dress.)* I think I'm going to go.

DAVID: Wait a minute. I'm ready. I'm ready now.

SUSAN: You don't have to prove anything to me.

DAVID: What "prove" anything? I'm not trying to prove anything. I'm trying to—

SUSAN: It was a pickup, David. I know what to expect.

DAVID: I thought we were getting along.

SUSAN: Please. Don't make me say anything to hurt your feelings…or make you hurt mine.

DAVID: Where did all of this hostility come from all of a sudden?

SUSAN: It's not hostility.

DAVID: What did I do?

SUSAN: Nothing.

DAVID: What?

SUSAN: I thought I was interested, okay? I changed my mind. Let's keep it at that.

(David starts out of bed, grabbing the sheet around his waist, moving to her.)

DAVID: Tell me what happened. I just want to know. What?

SUSAN: I don't want to say anymore.

DAVID: I want you to.

(He stops her from dressing.)

DAVID: What did I do?

SUSAN: When I showed initiative in bed, you backed away.

DAVID: Huh?

SUSAN: When I started to control our lovemaking you couldn't handle it and you backed away.

DAVID: I didn't back away, I—

SUSAN: I was asserting myself in bed. That's why—

DAVID: I didn't mean to—

SUSAN: That's why.

DAVID: Look…I was premature. Yeah, but…it had nothing to do with—

SUSAN: It was a punishment.

DAVID: No.

SUSAN: Tell me you didn't cum prematurely to punish me.

(There is a slight pause.)

DAVID: Okay. I'm sorry. If that's how it came across…I didn't mean for that to be my reaction…Okay? I surprised myself…I had a…whatever…a…reaction…it wasn't…I mean…I wasn't thinking that you needed to be punished.

SUSAN: What were you thinking then? Because that's what you did.

DAVID: Look, it was a reaction, it wasn't…uh…a purposeful thing. I couldn't help it. I don't know, maybe it was some…some…whateverthe…vestigial fucking…holdover…I don't…I wasn't consciously thinking anything…I wasn't feeling anything.

SUSAN: You weren't feeling anything?

DAVID: I don't mean it that way. What I mean is—

(She moves to leave. He stops her.)

DAVID: Will you just wait a minute.

SUSAN: For you and your vestigial…vestigial whatever…to do what?

DAVID: That was the wrong word.

SUSAN: Words, David. See? It's not about words. If I said I loved you…God, if I actually said that I had love for you, would you know how you'd feel? Forget about the words you'd use to describe it…would you even know the feeling?

(There is a pause. David cannot answer.)

SUSAN: Jesus.

DAVID: I know. I know when you look into your heart, you see this…whateverthefuck…range of feelings and emotions…and they're all easily…whateverthe…*differentiated* in front of you. But, when I look into mine, I don't see anything. Or if I do it's just this mass of…of…whateverthefuck…*mass* of…It scares the shit out of me, because I know there should be something that…that's…*recognizable*. But it's just…just…And all I have left is a choice. I can either keep quiet or fake it. And either way I lose with you. Because… you're going to be hurt if I don't say something…and you're going to think I'm holding back…or even worse…like…like I'm telling you of something by holding back. But…when I ask myself…when I look…I don't see anything… just a…whateverthefuck…mass of…of…*(There is a pause.)* What am I supposed to do with that?

SUSAN: You're breaking my heart, you know? You truly are.

July 7, 1994
Donald Marguiles

Scene: A community health center.

    1 Man and 1 Woman: Mr. Caridi (40s) patient and Kate (late 30s) doctor.

Kate works as a primary care physician in a community health center—she sees Mr. Caridi as a patient.

O   O   O

(Kate is with Mr. Caridi, an unstable, working-class man in his late 40s.)

KATE: What brings you here today, Mr. Caridi?

MR. CARIDI: You.

(She good-naturedly rolls her eyes.)

MR. CARIDI: No, I mean it, I been thinking about you. I *have;* that's the truth.

KATE: *(Over "that's the truth;" keeping her professional cool.)* Mr. Caridi, do you have a complaint?

MR. CARIDI: Only that I don't see you enough.

(Another disapproving look from Kate: she is not charmed.)

MR. CARIDI: What's the matter, I'm embarrassing you? A beautiful girl like you? Look at you, you're blushing.

KATE: I am not.

MR. CARIDI: Don't you know you're beautiful?

KATE: Come on, this is really…

MR. CARIDI: *(Over "this is really…")* Doesn't your husband tell you how beautiful you are? Boy, if you were *mine,* if you were *mine,* I'd tell you all the time, all the *time* I'd tell you.

KATE: *(Over "all the* time *I'd tell you.")* Mr. Caridi, do you have any idea how inappropriate this is? No honestly. Do you? I'm your *doctor,* Mr. Caridi.

MR. CARIDI: Hey…*(Meaning, "You don't have to tell me.")*

KATE: *(Continuous.)* Do you think you can respect that fact for ten minutes so that I can do my job?

MR. CARIDI: Shoot. *(Meaning, "Go ahead.")*

KATE: Thank you.

MR. CARIDI: *(Beat.)* Can I say one thing, though? You know?, in the beginning I really thought I was gonna have a problem having a lady doctor. But, no, I like it. I really do.

KATE: That's good, Mr. Caridi. I'm glad.

MR. CARIDI: There's something really nice about it, you know? Really refreshing.

KATE: Would you like to tell me what's wrong?

MR. CARIDI: *(Dead serious.)* I really have been thinking about you, you know. I missed you.

KATE: Mr. Caridi, this had got to stop. Okay? Because if you insist on this inappropriate behavior,—

MR. CARIDI: Don't get so worked up!

KATE: —I'm going to have to take you off my patient list and give you to Dr. Leventhal. Do you understand?

MR. CARIDI: Yes, Teacher—I mean, Doctor.

(He cracks himself up; she glares at him.)

MR. CARIDI: That was a joke! Come on! Where's your sense of humor?

KATE: Mr. Caridi, is there a medical reason that brought you here today?

MR. CARIDI: Yeah. What do you think, I make appointments just to see you?

(She says nothing.)

MR. CARIDI: I'm missing O.J. for this! Today's the big day!

KATE: Mr. Caridi, I'm already running twenty minutes late.

MR. CARIDI: Okay, okay, I see you're into being super-serious. I can be super-serious, too. *(He folds his hands like a student.)*

KATE: Well?

MR. CARIDI: I got a few things I care to discuss.

KATE: All right.

MR. CARIDI: Some personal matters.

KATE: Personal matters or health problems.

MR. CARIDI: Yeah. Health problems. *(Pause.)* You still want me to give up smoking?

KATE: Is that really why you're here? You want to talk about quitting smoking?—

MR. CARIDI: I know, I know.

KATE: *(Continuous.)* —We've talked about this before.

MR. CARIDI: I try. I really do. I just can't. The minute I decide to quit, I can't wait to light up again. Believe me, I'd be so happy to come and see you and tell you I quit. I couldn't wait to see the look on your face when I told you.

KATE: Maybe it's time to think about the patch.

MR. CARIDI: The what?

KATE: The nicotine patch. Remember?

MR. CARIDI: *(Shakes his head, No.)* What's that?

KATE: You wear it on your skin and it releases nicotine into your bloodstream. It takes away the craving.

MR. CARIDI: No kidding.

KATE: Would you like to try it?

MR. CARIDI: Yeah, sure, why not? Does it hurt?

KATE: No, you just wear it on your skin. Like a band-aid. Before you go I'll give you a starter kit. And then you'll need to fill this prescription. *(She writes.)* Okay?

MR. CARIDI: Yeah, Doc. Thanks. *(He watches her write in silence, refers to framed photo.)* That your kid?

KATE: What?

MR. CARIDI: *(Points to the photo.)* The kid.

KATE: Yes.

(Pause.)

MR. CARIDI: Can I see?

KATE: Mr. Caridi…

MR. CARIDI: Can't I see the picture? I just want to see it. I don't got my glasses. Can I see it up close? I love kids.

(She hesitates, then hands him the frame.)

MR. CARIDI: Thanks.

(He looks at the photo for a long time, which she finds terribly unnerving. She extends her hand.)

KATE: Mr. Caridi?

MR. CARIDI: So: that's your kid.

KATE: Yes. *(Beat.)* May I have it back, please?

MR. CARIDI: That your husband?

KATE: Yes.

MR. CARIDI: Pretty kid. What's his name?

KATE: *(Hesitates.)* Matthew.

MR. CARIDI: Matthew, huh.

KATE: May I please…?

MR. CARIDI: *(Still looking.)* Looks like you, don't he.

KATE: Mr. Caridi, please…Can we get on with this? I've got a whole bunch of patients I've got to see.

(Laughing, he taunts her with the picture frame.)

KATE: Mr. Caridi…Mr. Caridi, please…

(He gives it to her; she puts it back. Pause.)

MR. CARIDI: I wish I had that.

KATE: Had what?

MR. CARIDI: A kid, a family. Maybe if I had a kid…If I didn't have this…disability…Who knows? I might be sitting where you are. Or where your husband sits. You ever think about that? There but for the grace of God?

KATE: All the time. *(Beat.)* Mr. Caridi, have you been taking your lithium?

47

MR. CARIDI: Why?

KATE: I suspect you haven't.

MR. CARIDI: *(Beat.)* No.

KATE: Why not?

MR. CARIDI: *(Shrugs.)* I hate the way it makes me feel. Makes my mouth taste like shit.

KATE: You can always use a mouthwash if it dries out your mouth. Or chew gum. Mr. Caridi, you've got to be sure to tell your psychiatrist—when's your next appointment?

(He shrugs.)

KATE: Have you been going to your appointments?

MR. CARIDI: I don't like him. Why can't I see you?

KATE: I'm not a psychiatrist. Mr. Caridi, you've got to take your lithium and you've got to take it regularly, do you understand? You have bipolar *disease;*—

MR. CARIDI: Yeah yeah yeah.

KATE: *(Continuous.)* —it's a *disease,* controllable by drugs.

MR. CARIDI: *(Shrugs.)* I got another problem I got to ask you.

KATE: What kind of problem?

MR. CARIDI: It's kind of personal.

KATE: *(Beat.)* All right.

MR. CARIDI: Kind of confidential.

(She nods, "Okay.")

MR. CARIDI: You're my doctor, right?

KATE: Yes.

MR. CARIDI: I can discuss a personal problem with you, can't I? I mean, that's appropriate, isn't it? Hm? Doctor-patient thing? Like confession, right?

KATE: What's the problem, Mr. Caridi?

(Pause.)

MR. CARIDI: It's my penis.

KATE: *(Beat.)* Yes?

MR. CARIDI: I don't know, something don't seem right.

KATE: Can you be more specific?

MR. CARIDI: Sometimes...Sometimes I have this burning sensation.

KATE: It's painful when you urinate?

MR. CARIDI: I don't know, I think so. Yeah, it is. And sometimes it gets really big and red and swollen; I think you better take a look, Doc. *(He starts to undo his pants.)*

KATE: All right, all right, that's it.

MR. CARIDI: *(Feigning shock.)* What!

KATE: I did not tell you to take your pants down. *(His pants fall to his feet.)*

MR. CARIDI: Don't you want to see what's the matter?!—

KATE: Mr. Caridi…

MR. CARIDI: *(Continuous.)* —I tell you I got something wrong with my penis, don't you think you'd better take a look?! What's the matter, you shy? You're a doctor!; you've seen naked men before.

KATE: *(Over "naked men before.")* That's right, I'm not your friend, I'm not your girlfriend, I'm your doctor. Now put your pants back on before I call for help.

MR. CARIDI: *(His pants still around his ankles.)* How do you know there isn't something really wrong with me?!

KATE: You're right, I don't.

MR. CARIDI: *(Continuous.)* —How do you know I don't have cancer or a tumor or something?—

KATE: Mr. Caridi, pull up your pants, Mr. Caridi…

MR. CARIDI: *(Continuous.)* —What kind of doctor *are* you? Aren't you supposed to heal the sick? Aren't you?! You and Hillary Clinton! Phony bitches! All smiles and promises.

KATE: *(Overlap.)* I'm setting up another appointment for you with Dr. Leventhal.

MR. CARIDI: What?! Why?!

KATE: *(Continuous.)* I think Dr. Leventhal should be your primary care physician from now on. I think you need to see a male physician.

MR. CARIDI: Oh, come on! What kind of shit is this? What kind of doctor are you, anyway? You're no doctor. Where's your compassion? Doctors are supposed to have compassion.

KATE: Excuse me, I'll go get the patch. *(She leaves.)*

MR. CARIDI: Bitch.

(Pause. He picks up the picture frame to look at again, then impulsively hides it in his newspaper. She returns with the patch.)

KATE: Here, let me show you, all you do is…

(He snatches the patch from her.)

MR. CARIDI: *(As he goes.)* Suck my dick.

Kept Men
Richard Lay

Scene: New York City, the present
    1 Man and 1 Woman: Momma (50-60) a Mafia "Godmother" and Paulie (30s) her gay son.

Paulie has fallen in love with Phil, one of the mob's best hit men. Here he begs his gun-totin' Momma to let them be together.

O   O   O

PAULIE: *(Pleading.)* Momma, I have brought no dishonor on the family. I took the rap for poppa, I done 15 years in the joint and I woulda died in that stinking place had it not been for Phil. You can't understand Momma what it was like…locked up in my cell for 22 hours a day. I was goin' nuts until I met Phil. When we got out almost to the same day and you welcomed me back to the family, I pledged to Phil that I would always look after him and you must admit Momma that it went OK until last month.

MOMMA: Paulie, your father died of a broken heart when you told him you wanted to marry a man.

PAULIE: No, he didn't. He loved Phil. Poppa said I was the luckiest guy in the joint for having Phil look out for me. Momma, poppa died last month because that old bullet in his head moved a sixteenth-of-an-inch after all these years.

MOMMA: I'm not going to change my mind. Phil is out.

PAULIE: *(Stands and starts pacing.)* Phil happens to be the person I love. I love him like I love you.

MOMMA: Don't say that.

PAULIE: He also happens to be the best hit man since Sammy 'The Bull' Gravano. And you have to go and fire him.

MOMMA: Don't mention that name.

PAULIE: Sammy the Bull, Sammy the Bull, Sammy the Bull! Momma, it embarrasses me to pick up the New York *Post* and the *Daily News* and see pictures of you on the front page with headlines shouting "Maria Gambuto—New York's Godmother." They are putting you up there with John Gotti, Paul Castellano…Lucky Luciano.

MOMMA: Al Capone? *(Smiles contentedly.)*

PAULIE: Al Capone…Mamma we got a be discreet.

MOMMA: *(Pause.)* Your friend Phil. I've made him redundant. You must find a nice girl because one day you will be the head of the Family.

PAULIE: But momma, I love him. I know if you just went home to Palermo and stayed with Uncle Guiseppe and got a suntan and looked after the olive oil farms, you would be far happier. Me and Phil with a few cops in our pocket, some muscle on the streets, my brains and Phil's penchant for popping the right people…it will be a new era.

MOMMA: Palermo. *(Dreamily.)* That's where both of your grandfathers were born. I was there once when I was 14. Just pronouncing the word P A L E R M O. You know your father could make the word last 12 seconds. Try it.

PAULIE: I believe you.

MOMMA: How long have you liked men?

PAULIE: How long have I…?

MOMMA: I'm not sure I *ever* did. Your father was not a nice man. But you know that. I never saw you as a man. You have always been my baby Paulie. On cold nights when your father was away stealing from the airports you must have been 12—you could never sleep. Your brain was too busy. You would creep along the landing and snuggle in with me. Your father said it was unnatural—but we were so warm and snug. Maybe he was right. Maybe all this is my fault.

PAULIE: I remember Momma. I would stay awake so that I could sleep with you. It didn't seem wrong. It seemed natural. It seemed the only thing to do.

MOMMA: *(Softer.)* This Phil. He really does mean a lot to you doesn't he?

PAULIE: Everything.

MOMMA: And he whacks well?

PAULIE: The very best.

MOMMA: I got an idea. Maybe this will work, cos I love you Paulie and I want you to be happy, very happy. Your poppa had a dying wish.

PAULIE: He did?

MOMMA: He was worried. Since the Feds and New York's Organized Crime Squad took out Johnnie Gotti and a lot of very nice people I met at weddings and funerals for years, things have been tougher…Tighter. Your father was one of the last of the few who really cared for the old traditions. What worried him was that the Organized Crime Squad had him as the next target. He died a worried man and I inherit his concerns. He said the only way to deal with things was to take out the person who was after you—don't matter if it's Fed or NYPD. I will turn a blind eye with you…and Phil, if Phil can take out the person your father feared most.

PAULIE: Momma, just give me a name.

(He leans in close to her mouth and she whispers.)

MOMMA: Now we have other business to attend to, bring him out.

Living In Paradise

Jack Gilhooley

Scene: A college dorm room

    1 Man and 1 Woman: Butch (16) a precocious college freshman and Max (20) his brother's girlfriend.

Butch has just started his freshman year and is perplexed by the fact that one of his professors walked into class dressed like a geisha. Here, he visits Max with whom he shares insights and revelations.

○   ○   ○

MAX: Huh?

BUTCH: I didn't say anything.

MAX: You said…you asked if he was going "to look at the pictures."

BUTCH: I think he said something about an art gallery.

MAX: Bullshit! He's never been to an art gallery in his life. He's going to the courthouse. To see the photographs.

BUTCH: I think he was kidding.

MAX: That…*ghoul!!!! (She leaps up and tears the door open, shouting…) Harry!…Harry! (After a moment, she re-enters and closes the door dejectedly…)* He didn't. How could he? Why would he want to see those photographs?

BUTCH: He said he was taking a criminology course. An elective. Said it was a class assignment.

MAX: Bullshit! He's a business major. Why would he want to take a criminology course?

BUTCH: *(Shrugs.)* To learn business ethics. Why did he take an acting course?

MAX: For poise. He sees a life in the public eye. TV…personal appearances… Despite what you may think, your brother's one shrewd dude. He took it for assurance…poise…

BUTCH: And for you.

MAX: Huh?

BUTCH: He told us he took the course to get close to you.

MAX: He said that?

BUTCH: You surprised? My father said, "Why're you taking a 'faggot' acting course?"

MAX: Am I surprised? I'm skeptical. You know your brother. He can be charming…he's handsome and he's gonna get rich. Every move he makes is calculated.

BUTCH: You don't love him?

MAX: None of your business, sonny. *(Pause. She stammers and then blurts out…)* Look, with my family fidelity was not a priority item. Especially my father. I mean to say, my father's cheating affected my mother. And Mother was never one to take things lying down. Although, that's exactly what she did. Harry's got that jock morality (if that's not an oxymoron). I know what those guys do on the road. Here at home, for that matter. A year from now, Harry will be gone…playing ball…bucks in his pocket. He won't even call. I'm dead meat.

BUTCH: Wrong.

MAX: We've never even talked about our future. Maybe it's just as well. I'm not sure I want one.

BUTCH: You don't want a future?

MAX: With Harry? *(Beat.)* Maybe. I dunno. *(Beat.)* Why am I telling you this?

BUTCH: You want it to get back to him? I'd love for it to get back to him. I'd deliver the message. Free of charge. "Harry, Max is not interested in an insensitive jock who gets off on atrocity pictures." Of course, I'd phone the message in.

MAX: Forget I said anything.

BUTCH: Done! My lips are sealed. I'd never violate your trust in me. Assuming you have some. I reckon I'd die before I'd rat on you.

MAX: I think we're on the rocks, anyway. We don't need a hatchet man.

BUTCH: *(Semi-proudly.)* Hatchet man? Me?

MAX: Why do you say "reckon" all the time? Is that how they talk in Lauderdale?

BUTCH: I don't reckon so. I'm tryna develop…well…an identity. I was born in the deep South but—

BUTCH: I thought you were born in Florida.

BUTCH: That's what I'm talking about. I was born in the southern part of the most southern state. But people don't think of it as "deep South." No hominy grits…no moonshine…no Dixieland. Why is it that people north of here are more Southern? And as you travel further South, it gets more Northern…Northeastern, in fact. Does that bother you?

MAX: Not in the least. I never think of it.

BUTCH: Most folks from my hometown are New Yorkers or New Englanders or Cubans. The trouble with my hometown is…well, I guess you've heard of

Gertrude Stein. She sort of summed it up. She said, "There's no there, there." Well, you're more than just a scientist if you know her work.

BUTCH: I don't know her work. I only know her phrase. And I'm not sure what it's supposed to mean. But I know what she's saying. If that's not a contradiction.

MAX: It is. But it's OK. I feel the same way about you. I don't always know what you mean but I think I know what you're saying.

BUTCH: I'm a pretty complex kid.

MAX: No, basically inarticulate. And Stein said it about Oakland.

BUTCH: She said it about Ft. Lauderdale, too. She just never knew it. I say "reckon" to give myself a sense of place. Even if I'm the only one in the place that says it. They don't have accents back home. They don't sound Southern. The only distinctive accent is Spanish. But I can't walk around saying, "I teeeddnk I go to theee movieees."

MAX: *You* could, Butch. No one would bat an eye.

BUTCH: I'd rather people think I'm a little strange than not think about me at all. Why did you come all the way here from California? It can't be the weather.

MAX: It's the distance.

BUTCH: Oh…I see.

MAX: No, you don't.

BUTCH: You're right. Explain, please.

MAX: Say what you mean, Butch. You wanna grow up to be like your brother?

BUTCH: Well, yeah. In some ways. But it's too late. I am grown up and I'm *not* like him.

MAX: In that case, I'll try to help you. I'm chaperoning the freshman social on Friday.

BUTCH: I don't socialize very well. But if you'll be there…

MAX: Would you like to meet a girl?

BUTCH: Lots of them. I had acne until this summer. I was lucky. I got over it early. Most kids have it a long time. I'd like to have the Clearasil franchise on this campus. I'd always been self-conscious about it. I'd talk with my head down. Girls could converse with the top of my cranium…if they'd converse at all.

(She removes his cap, examines his hair.)

MAX: You have nice hair. If they didn't have to talk to this stupid cap, you might have had a girlfriend.

(She tosses the hat across the room. He doesn't retrieve it.)

BUTCH: Does Harry come up here very often?

54

MAX: Sometimes we'd go to his room.

BUTCH: What about his roommate?

MAX: When his roommate was at his girlfriend's place.

BUTCH: I see. Musical beds. College can be fun for some guys. "Was"? You don't go to his room anymore?

MAX: I just got back. Two days ago. And I haven't been invited.

BUTCH: Well, if you want me to put a bug in his ear then—

MAX: Never mind. Time to go.

BUTCH: You don't love him.

(She steers him to the door as graciously as possible. He fetches his cap.)

MAX: Butch, I wanna take a nap.

BUTCH: *(Reluctant to leave.)* If you don't love him, you're wasting your time with Harry.

MAX: Butch...enough.

BUTCH: I mean, he's got attributes. I'll grant you.

(She's opened the door.)

MAX: You've got attributes of your own.

BUTCH: I've a bigger pecker.

MAX: *(Truly unamused.)* Oh, by all means, get back in here!

BUTCH: *(Dumbstruck paralysis.)* Are...are you...serious?

MAX: In your dreams, *idiot!!!* Hit the road!!!

(Physically steering him out the door, he offers slight resistance...)

BUTCH: OK, I'm going. *(Stepping out.)* Are you mad at me?

MAX: I'm mad at your brother for leaving you here.

(She slams the door but it bounces off of Butch who howls...)

BUTCH: Owwwwwwwwwww!

(She's alarmed and concerned since he's holding his forehead in great pain. She readmits him.)

MAX: Oh, God...I'm sorry. I'm so sorry. Let me see.

(He removes his hand from his head. He seems in genuine pain.)

MAX: It's not bleeding.

BUTCH: Oh, thanks a lot, Max. I don't think I deserved that. I think I've got a concussion.

MAX: Well, at least it wasn't your humongous peck—

BUTCH: I could press charges. But I won't.

MAX: Go ahead. I'll countercharge. I'll say you tried to rape me. I hit you with a chair. I'd win, hands down. Nobody would believe that I'd willingly let *you* in my room.

BUTCH: Boy, you can really be a bitch.

MAX: You don't want to press charges, then. You're a strange boy.

BUTCH: Before I go can I ask you opinion?

MAX: Nothing personal.

BUTCH: Promise…Why a geisha?

MAX: Who knows? Except Corello. Maybe his wife had something to do with it.

BUTCH: Maybe his wife *was* a geisha.

MAX: *(Without conviction.)* That's it. That's the answer.

BUTCH: Not for me, it's not. If he dresses like a geisha cause his wife was a geisha…well…I mean, if I got married to a stripper—a rather unlikely prospect for any self-respecting stripper—

MAX: Then *you* would hardly walk around in a G-string.

BUTCH: Exactly. You read my mind.

MAX: I don't read smut.

BUTCH: It's gotta be something else. Well, I'm sorry I messed up your day. Don't believe everything Harry tells you.

MAX: About you?

BUTCH: About anything. On Friday, Max, I'd appreciate it if you'd steer me to an aggressive-type girl.

MAX: Aggressive women turn most guys off.

BUTCH: Not me. I'm not most guys.

MAX: Tell me about it.

BUTCH: If she's not aggressive, nothing's gonna happen. I'm shy.

MAX: How's your head?

BUTCH: No problem. It wasn't my head. I put my foot in the door.

(Max shakes her head in quasi despair.)

MAX: Shy?

BUTCH: Don't be pissed. I just wanted more time with you. Well, so long, Maxine.

MAX: See ya, Butch.

(He leans in and kisses her on the cheek. She reciprocates. When he starts to get slightly intimate, she withdraws without offense.)

BUTCH: I wouldn't've done that a few months ago. Before my skin cleared up. I'd kiss Martha and she'd flinch. Y'know, it was just a sort of "cousinly" kiss. I wasn't gonna stick my tongue down a relative's throat. Martha can ill-afford to look a gift horse in the mouth. It was only a horde of zits. They didn't bite. Anyway, so long.

MAX: So long again, Butch.

The Monogamist

Christopher Kyle

Scene: New York City during the Bush administration
    1 Man and 1 Woman: Dennis (40) a poet going through a midlife crisis and Susan (35) his
    long-suffering wife.

*When Dennis discovers Susan in bed with one of her students, he moves out of their home and
into his NYC studio. Here, the estranged couple meet at a sidewalk cafe to discuss their future.*

O   O   O

*(Susan and Dennis at a sidewalk cafe in New York. Cups of cappuccino in
front of them. Dennis is fishing for something in his bag.)*
DENNIS: How are you?
SUSAN: I'm fine, Dennis. Did you order anything to eat?
DENNIS: No. Would you like something?
SUSAN: I meant for you. You don't look like you've been eating; you're pale.
DENNIS: I always look like this in sunlight.
SUSAN: Thank you for seeing me, Dennis. I understand how you must feel
right now, but I think we need to talk.
DENNIS: I've been wanting to talk to you.
SUSAN: Really? That's good. *(Beat.)* I'd like us to get back together, if we can.
Or at least talk about the possibility.
(Dennis takes the tape recorder out of his bag and puts it on the table.)
SUSAN: What's this?
DENNIS: It's my tape recorder. Do you mind if I tape this? I find it therapeutic.
I've been taping all my thoughts and conversations lately. Then when I lis-
ten, sometimes I can detect things.
SUSAN: Things?
DENNIS: Yes. Clues.
SUSAN: *(Beat.)* I'd rather not be taped, thank you.
DENNIS: I promise you, I'm not doing it on the advice of an attorney or any-
thing like that. It's for my personal use only.
SUSAN: Can't we just talk?
DENNIS: That's exactly what I want to do. What if I tape what I say and then
press the pause button while you're talking?
(Pause.)
SUSAN: Dennis, what's wrong with you?
DENNIS: Nothing's wrong with me. I just miss things, you know, I forget—
things I want to remember. Like the other day I was remembering when we

first met—licking envelopes for the Carter campaign—and how we went back to my apartment and all I had to drink was Pernod and you really hated it but I could tell we were going to get along because you pretended to like it. And I tried to kiss you much sooner than I'd ever tried to kiss anyone before—I mean, I barely knew your last name—but you kissed me back as if you'd been waiting for hours, years even. And I knew that moment I wanted to be with you forever.

SUSAN: I remember.

DENNIS: But don't you wish we had it on tape?

SUSAN: I'm sorry?

DENNIS: I mean, after all that's happened since then, wouldn't it be wonderful if we could see what we had back then? Maybe we'd understand how everything went wrong.

SUSAN: Are you serious?

DENNIS: Absolutely. That's why I think it's so important that we record this conversation.

SUSAN: *(Beat.)* Dennis, I came to talk to you about our relationship, because I'd like to think there's a chance we can put it back together. But if you don't put that tape recorder away, I'm going to leave.

DENNIS: You really feel that strongly about it?

SUSAN: I really do.

(He puts away the tape recorder.)

DENNIS: I'm planning to get a voice-activated recorder, anyway. It's less obtrusive.

(Pause.)

SUSAN: How have you been?

DENNIS: Great. I really like staying in New York full-time, you know. Princeton's so bogus.

SUSAN: Bogus? Since when do you say "bogus," Dennis?

DENNIS: Must've picked it up somewhere. Do you know any young people, Susan? Aside from Tim.

SUSAN: I'm a teacher, Dennis. I have four sections of young people.

DENNIS: Because I met a young person the other night. Her name is Sky.

SUSAN: I see.

DENNIS: It was very frightening at first. She's a Republican.

SUSAN: They're all Republicans, Dennis. They're taking revenge on their hippie parents.

DENNIS: She's not *really* a Republican—she doesn't grasp the issues well enough to be ideological about anything. But she's so open, you know? It was marvelous the way she reacted when I was telling her my theory of how the very smallest act can have political ramifications. It was an awakening.

SUSAN: You fell in love with her.

DENNIS: Do you think so?

SUSAN: I don't know. I'm asking. You fell in love with her, didn't you?

DENNIS: Do you think she's too young for me? She's about Tim's age.

SUSAN: All right, Dennis, if you're going to be hostile—

DENNIS: It's funny—she looks just like you did in the 70s: tie-dye, beads, every-thing.

SUSAN: Dennis, please.

DENNIS: I gave her Pernod.

(Pause.)

SUSAN: I see.

DENNIS: She didn't like it, either.

SUSAN: Look, I'm sorry I hurt you, Dennis—

DENNIS: That makes two of us.

SUSAN: But I think it's childish to play these tit-for-tat games. So you slept with some chirpy little peacenik wannabe. Fine. We're even. Now could we please talk about what happens next?

DENNIS: Next?

SUSAN: What's going to happen with us?

DENNIS: Well, I don't know. I think I have real feelings for Sky.

SUSAN: Don't be ridiculous.

DENNIS: I'm very serious. I haven't felt this way in, well, fifteen years.

SUSAN: So you and this—this—Cloud—

DENNIS: Sky.

SUSAN: You're going to move in together or something?

DENNIS: We already have.

SUSAN: Already? I can't believe you! What happened to Mr. Monogamy?

DENNIS: As you know, Susan, I staked an entire book on that proposition only to find my wife in the arms of an unapologetic sexist twenty years my junior.

SUSAN: I'm sorry, Dennis. But maybe monogamy is something you have to work at, did you ever think of that?

DENNIS: I've done nothing but work at it, Susan. Then one day I walk into my bedroom and find you with Tim and all that work goes right down the toi-let. So now I'm going to try and rediscover whatever it was we used to have.

SUSAN: With this girl?

DENNIS: Yes.

SUSAN: So that's it, then? It's over.

DENNIS: I think so. *(Pause.)* Are you still seeing Tim?

SUSAN: Of course. I mean, I could be. He's still *interested* in me. But I thought after we talked…

DENNIS: He seems like a nice guy.

SUSAN: He's moving in.

DENNIS: Into our house?

SUSAN: Yes.

DENNIS: Well, I'm sure you know best.

SUSAN: Does that bother you?

DENNIS: I don't see why it would.

SUSAN: Because obviously this is what we both want, isn't it? I guess we were just waiting for a catalyst.

DENNIS: Obviously.

SUSAN: I'm certainly tired of propping up a neurotic, self-absorbed artist morning, noon and night. I don't think you have the slightest idea how much you demand of me.

DENNIS: You think I'm neurotic?

SUSAN: Besides, I'm thirty-five years old, Dennis, and I want to have a baby before it's too late.

DENNIS: I wouldn't be good with a baby. I think one of my strengths is that I never grew up. Being a parent would kill that.

SUSAN: Exactly. It's so clear we want such different things, Dennis. I don't know why it's taken us so long to see it. *(Beat.)* And you know what? Tim really loves kids. He'd make a wonderful father. *(She rises, gathering her things.)* I guess that's all that needs to be said, isn't it? I'm asking Carol to be my attorney.

DENNIS: Who am I supposed to get?

SUSAN: I'm sure you'll find someone. She's not the only lawyer around.

DENNIS: *(Rising.)* It doesn't matter. I don't want anything. Take it. You can have my books. Everything. I don't want to set foot in that house again.

SUSAN: We'll be more than fair, Dennis.

DENNIS: I'm sure you will. You and Tim and Carol.

SUSAN: Well. Good-bye. *(She starts to leave.)*

DENNIS: Susan? I just want you to know, I've been working almost nonstop since I moved out. I'm quite capable of creating on my own.

SUSAN: Do you really think so? For such a long time I deluded myself with the idea that you enjoyed having me around. *(Pause.)* Good-bye, Dennis.

(She exits. Pause. Dennis slumps back into his seat. He gets out his tape recorder and begins talking.)

DENNIS: I'm in a cafe on Amsterdam near one-tenth. Susan and I have decided to get a divorce…I can't really think of anything to say right now. I'm thinking of when all those kids in Cincinnati got trampled waiting for the Who concert. I feel trampled.

The Queen's Knight
Frank Cossa

Scene: Paris, October, 1793
    1 Man and 1 Woman: Jacques Hebert, Assistant Prosecutor of the Revolutionary Tribunal and Marie-Antoinette, the former Queen of France.

Marie-Antoinette stands before the Tribunal accused of many crimes, including having sent two-hundred million francs to her brother, the Emperor Joseph of Austria, for use in his war with Turkey. When questioned on this point by Hebert, the former Queen unwittingly opens herself up to an attack of a more personal nature.

O   O   O

HEBERT: *(To Queen.)* What have you to say to this charge, Madame?

QUEEN: Ridiculous. I never had such money.

HEBERT: How much did you send to Austria?

QUEEN: Nothing.

HEBERT: Nothing? Your brother was at war and you sent him nothing?

QUEEN: That's correct.

HEBERT: Where did you send money?

QUEEN: Foreign loans were made only with the consent of the government.

HEBERT: Loans to whom?

QUEEN: To the English colonies in America when they were in revolt.

HEBERT: How much?

QUEEN: I don't know.

HEBERT: Why was this money sent there?

QUEEN: To aid the revolt.

HEBERT: Why?

QUEEN: It was in the interest of France.

HEBERT: How?

QUEEN: I don't know. The ministers of state decided these things. I didn't always understand.

HEBERT: You supported this decision, did you not?

QUEEN: Yes.

HEBERT: Yet you did not understand what you were supporting? You took money from an already depleted treasury and sent it away while the people of your own country were starving. And you didn't even understand why?

QUEEN: No, I...but—

HEBERT: *(Playing to the gallery.)* You were told, were you not, that your people had no bread?

QUEEN: I did not understand—

HEBERT: And you answered, did you not, "Let them eat cake!"

QUEEN: No! I never said that! It isn't true!

HEBERT: Well, Madame?

QUEEN: Many Frenchmen were going to America to fight—

HEBERT: *(Seizing on this.)* Yes. Aristocrats. Your friends, your lovers. Was not the Count Fersen among them? Did he not persuade you to send money to America?

QUEEN: No…yes…he did go, but he did not persuade me—

HEBERT: He didn't have to. You wished to protect your lover. You provided him with a regiment of troops.

QUEEN: No…that is…he was not my lover. Of course he commanded troops.

HEBERT: Given him by you.

QUEEN: He was qualified.

HEBERT: Was he? What was his battle experience?

QUEEN: He was…in Sweden…

HEBERT: There was no war in Sweden, Madame, as there was no war in the bordellos of Paris which he frequented. He had no battle experience! And what feats of arms did he perform in America?

QUEEN: *(Clearly shaken and flustered.)* He was…very brave, I'm told.

HEBERT: Brave indeed. He promptly became ill, languished in bed for some months, and sailed bravely home.

QUEEN: No, that is not—

HEBERT: Where he was given a hero's welcome and a rich reward in money and titles, by you, Madame. Because he was your lover!

QUEEN: No. He was not!

HEBERT: Did he not visit you at night in your apartments by a private stairway?

QUEEN: *(Hesitates.)* Yes.

HEBERT: Speak up, Madame, did he or did he not?

QUEEN: Yes.

HEBERT: Why?

QUEEN: He came to…advise me.

HEBERT: I was under the impression, Madame, that ministers of state met with the King and Queen by daylight, in the Council Chambers at Versailles. Not in the middle of the night in the Queen's boudoir with the King conspicuously absent.

QUEEN: Count Fersen was not a minister of the State.

HEBERT: What was he?

QUEEN: A personal friend and advisor.

HEBERT: Why did you need a foreign advisor?

QUEEN: I trusted him.

HEBERT: To do what? Carry out your intrigues with foreign courts? Your plots against the interests of France?

QUEEN: No.

HEBERT: Or was it merely that he was a handsome and virile and a notorious rake that excited you?

QUEEN: No.

HEBERT: Admit it, Madame, Count Fersen was the father of your children.

QUEEN: No!

HEBERT: Who was?

QUEEN: My husband. King Louis the Sixteenth of France.

HEBERT: The Comte d'Artois?

QUEEN: No!

HEBERT: Why did he say he was?

QUEEN: He lied!

HEBERT: Why?

QUEEN: I don't know. Because it amused him.

HEBERT: He was your husband's brother. A brother wouldn't say such a thing if it weren't true.

QUEEN: A brother wouldn't say such a thing at all!

HEBERT: *(Taking a sheet of paper from his desk.)* Madame, I will read to you a list of names. Kindly indicate which of them were your lovers. They are in alphabetical rather than chronological order. I hope this won't confuse you. The Comte d'Artois.

QUEEN: No.

HEBERT: The Duc de Coigny.

QUEEN: No.

HEBERT: Edouard Dillon.

QUEEN: No.

HEBERT: The English Ambassador, The Duc de Dorset.

QUEEN: No.

HEBERT: Count Fersen.

QUEEN: No.

HEBERT: The Duc de Guines.

QUEEN: No.

HEBERT: Prince George de Hesse-Darmstadt.

QUEEN: No.

HEBERT: Lambertye, an officer of the Guard.

QUEEN: No.

HEBERT: The Duc de Liaincourt.

QUEEN: No.

HEBERT: The Duc de Polignac.

QUEEN: No.

HEBERT: Cardinal de Rohan.

QUEEN: No.

HEBERT: Comte de Romanzof.

QUEEN: No.

HEBERT: Comte de Vaudreuil.

QUEEN: No.

(Herbert folds paper.)

QUEEN: My son is legitimate, Monsieur.

HEBERT: And you wish to see him regain his throne, do you not?

QUEEN: I wish only what is best for the people of France.

HEBERT: Of course.

Rain

Garry Williams

Scene: Present, dusk, farmhouse porch
    1 Man and 1 Woman: Staff (40s) ex-farmer recently injured and now confined to a wheel-chair and Mary (40s) a once-pretty farmer's wife.

Mary and Staff's 17-year-old daughter has just left in the family car to "go out." The parents have differing attitudes about it.

O   O   O

(The silence descends once again. Mary continues with her knitting. Staff sighs heavily. He studies the sky for awhile.)

STAFF: Okay, let's have it.

(Nothing from Mary.)

STAFF: Let's just get it over with okay?

MARY: Why?

STAFF: Because I don't want to sit here and listen to you knit all night.

MARY: You tried to make me mad, you made me mad. Why do we have to talk about it?

STAFF: I didn't try to make you mad.

MARY: Sure you did.

STAFF: I kept you from hounding her. If that makes you mad, it'll just have to be that way.

MARY: Fine. I'm not supposed to be concerned about my daughter. How silly of me not to realize that.

STAFF: Being concerned is one thing. Making her life hell is another.

MARY: Making her life…?? Now, if that isn't the…What in the world do my fears have to do with—

STAFF: Your *fears?* What do you fear?

MARY: Now, don't go picking my words apart.

STAFF: What are your fears? What are you afraid of for Lindy tonight?

MARY: Staff, don't pick a fight, okay?

STAFF: I just want to know what you fear for our daughter.

MARY: She's a young girl, what do you think I fear?

STAFF: Youth?

MARY: Now, stop.

STAFF: Put a name to it. Call it by name and maybe it'll go away.

MARY: Don't be silly.

STAFF: Isn't that what Jesus did? Didn't he find out the name of some devil and cast it out? Name it, Mary.

MARY: I'm not going to say it out loud, if that's what you want.

STAFF: Death? Is that the big fear? You afraid she's going to die tonight?

MARY: Don't even say that.

STAFF: Just trying to help here.

MARY: Well, stop.

STAFF: How about unhappiness? You afraid of that for her?

MARY: Of course I want her to be happy. What kind of question is that?

STAFF: Loneliness? That one of them?

MARY: Let's just drop it, okay?

STAFF: I want to know what you're afraid of.

MARY: All of it! I'm her mother!

(Staff throws his head back and laughs.)

STAFF: Damn big job.

MARY: Yes it is.

(There is a lengthy silence. Staff starts in again. He is serious, but there is also an undercurrent of plain mischief.)

STAFF: Want me to tell you what you're really afraid of?

MARY: No.

STAFF: Why not?

MARY: Because it's going to be hateful. And it won't be right, either.

STAFF: Oh, it'll be right, all right.

MARY: Well, don't anyway.

STAFF: Sure you don't want to know? Might clarify some things for you.

MARY: You don't need to tell me.

STAFF: Might help, though.

MARY: No it won't.

STAFF: Sex.

(Mary closes her eyes for a moment. Then she puts her knitting on the couch and stands.)

MARY: I'm going in. Come on, Tyler, let's see if *Alf* is on yet.

STAFF: *(Rolling back to block the door.)* That's really your fear, isn't it.

MARY: No, for your information, it's not. The discussion is closed.

(Unable to get to the door, she storms over to the empty basket, carries it to the clothesline. Dry or not, she starts yanking clothes down and folding them with a fury.)

STAFF: She walked out of here and all you could see was her out in the back seat with some yahoo farmboy.

MARY: You stop this right now.

STAFF: You know it's true. You'd like to be worried about something worthwhile like her physical safety or state of mind. But when you get right down to it, your big concern is what she's out there doing with her private parts! You might as well just admit it.

MARY: *(Stuffing clothes in the basket.)* That isn't all I'm worried about, Staff.

STAFF: The hell it isn't. What was your mental image when she left here?

MARY: My what?

STAFF: Your mental image. What were you picturing?

MARY: Staff, now quit, I mean it.

STAFF: You were picturing her going at it with some kid, weren't you.

MARY: You're being stupid now.

STAFF: You were. You know you were.

MARY: You think that isn't tied up with the rest of it? You think she'll be happy if she gets pregnant? You think she won't be lonely if none of her friends have anything to do with her? You worry about one thing and you're worrying about the rest. It works that way, Staff.

STAFF: How far'd you take it?

MARY: Take what?

STAFF: This night of unbridled lust. You've already got her a pregnant outcast, how much farther did you go?

MARY: That's not…

STAFF: Did she die? Some back alley abortion kill her, did it?

MARY: Stop it now! I mean it, Staff!

STAFF: And of course that's not all the farther we can take it, is it. Oh, no, not even death can stop our worries. We've got the everlasting soul to think about—

MARY: *(Almost a scream.)* Stop it!

Tough Choices for the New Century
Jane Anderson

Scene: Southern California, Present
1 Man and 1 Woman: Bob Dooley (30s-40s and Arden Shingles (30s).

Arden is a self-defense expert at Bob's seminar on personal safety. Here they focus on women's safety and femininity.

ARDEN: There you go. I know a lot of women who are ready to take responsibility for their own protection, but they say to me, "Arden, I just can't get behind using a gun." And that's a very natural reaction. As women, our traditional role has been to be life giver, not life taker. Yes, I agree with all of that. But as life giver, what am I going to do when there's been a hurricane, all lines of communication are down, my husband has gone off to find supplies, and a strange man has just kicked down my door?
(Arden picks up a ring of keys from the table, fits them between her fingers. Bob joins her for a demonstration.)
ARDEN: Here's a good one. How many of you have thought of this? "OK, I'm now going to defend myself with a bunch of keys sticking out of my knuckles."
BOB: "Watch out, I'm going to kill you, Lady."
(Bob does a simulated attack, disarms Arden then holds her in a grip.)
ARDEN: *(To audience.)* Now what? I am now free to be raped, disfigured and killed.
(Arden taps Bob to let him know to release her. Arden picks up a can of mace.)
ARDEN: OK, that didn't work, what if I keep a can of mace in my emergency supply box. Here goes.
BOB: "I'm going to kill you, Lady."
(Arden holds up the can of mace, pretends to spray. Bob coughs twice then grabs Arden, holds her in the same grip.)
ARDEN: Oops, guess no one told me that most mace sold on the market is so diluted that it's about as effective as a baby peeing on a rabid dog. Again, I am now free to be raped, disfigured and killed.
(Arden taps Bob. He releases his grip. Arden picks up a stun gun.)

ARDEN: OK, that was fun, now that all my broken ribs are healed and I've got most of my face back, I think I'll buy myself a stun gun. Now this is a great weapon. It won't penetrate a heavy coat or a leather jacket and in order for it to work at all you have to hold it against the struggling body of your two-hundred-pound assailant for a full three seconds.

BOB: "Bitch! I'm going to kill you, Bitch."

(Arden looks a bit surprised by Bob's acting, then continues the demonstration, tries to zap Bob. Bob grabs her arms holds the gun away from his body then throws Arden into a grip, holding the stun gun next to one of her nipples.)

ARDEN: Once again, it's open season on me. All right.

(Arden taps Bob. It takes him a little longer to release her this time. Bob starts to walk back to his chair. Bob suddenly rushes back at Arden. Arden grabs a gun from the table, and whips around taking a stance.)

ARDEN: "Stop right there. Advance any further and I'll shoot."

(Bob immediately stops.)

ARDEN: "Slowly back away with your hands up. If you make any other movement I will kill you."

BOB: "Don't hurt me, Lady, please don't hurt me."

(Arden backs Bob up and makes him sit in the chair. She lowers the gun and walks back to the table, puts the gun back down.)

ARDEN: Which method of defense involved no physical contact between you and your assailant? Which method of defense protected your dignity as well as your life? And which method of defense involved the least amount of violence? It's like when we used to have nuclear weapons between us and the Russians, which I think was one of the biggest deterrents to war ever. In other words: the more *effective* your weapon is, the *less likely* you will have to use it. What we're talking about is deterrence, Folks. Not death, *deterrence*.

BOB: It's like preparedness.

ARDEN: That's right. See, I get crazy when people just make these blanket assumptions that all guns kill. That's like saying , "oh, let's get rid of all cars because of all the highway deaths." Hey, fine with me—did you know that there are twenty times more fatalities caused by cars than by guns? And you don't see Car Control lobbies out there in Washington. You don't see anyone instituting a ten-day waiting period before you can purchase your new VW. What do you drive, Bob?

BOB: A Ford Bronco.

ARDEN: You like to buy American?

BOB: Wouldn't buy anything else.

ARDEN: Where are all our guns manufactured, Bob?

BOB: The good ol' U.S. of A.

ARDEN: There you go. *(To audience.)* But it all comes down to this: deterrence equals power, power equals choice, choice equals life. By the way, the first thing Hitler did when he came into power? He took the guns away from the Jewish people. All things to think about. Whoever has the gun, would you mind holding it up so Bob can collect it?

(Bob walks down to the audience. Arden sits on the edge of the table.)

ARDEN: Isn't life funny? Lemme tell you one last story. I remember when I was a little girl, my family and I took a trip to the New York World's Fair. Anybody remember going to that? Anyway, there was this one exhibit called The City of Tomorrow. We stood in this long line that went into a room where you stood on a catwalk and looked down at a giant model of what a city would look like in fifty years. There were all these dome-shaped houses and weird-looking towers and monorails. And all the little people in the city looked kind of sealed in…and I don't know it all looked so strange to me that I got a sick feeling in my stomach. I started to cry and my mother asked me what the problem was. I told her my stomach hurt and she said that was because I'd been eating junk all day. And I said, "no, my stomach hurt because the model of The City of Tomorrow scared me, that I didn't ever want to have to live like that." And my father looked down at me, and you know what he said? He said, "Don't worry, Girl, by the time the future gets here, you won't know the difference."

(Bob hands Arden the .38 and a case of bullets. She slowly starts loading bullets into the gun.)

ARDEN: One last point. What would happen if I put bullets in this gun and passed it back around? *(A beat.)* Maybe that gun would just continue to be passed from hand to hand. Or maybe it would stop with that one bad apple who's sitting among you. He or she would hold on to that loaded gun, cock the hammer and take advantage of us one by one. *(A beat.)* OK, but what if I gave everyone a loaded gun? You see how it all makes sense?

(Arden hands the loaded gun back to Bob. She exits.)

BOB: OK, folks. A lot to think about. We're going to take a short break. Stretch your legs, there's drinks in the lobby. We'll see you back in fifteen.

(Bob puts the loaded gun in the case and snaps it shut. He picks it up and exits.)

Twelve Dreams

James Lapine

Scene: A university town in New England, 1936
   1 Man and 1 Woman: Sanford Putnam (20-30) a student of psychiatry and Miss Banton (20-30) a teacher of dance.

Putnam has dwelled too long in the dry (and male-dominated) world of academic psychiatry as may be seen in the following scene in which the bookish young man first encounters the attractive Miss Banton.

○   ○   ○

BANTON: What a wonderful movie. Pasteur was such a great man. Imagine making those contributions in your lifetime.

PUTNAM: Uh huh.

BANTON: Science is so marvelous.

PUTNAM: Mmmmmm.

BANTON: I love Paul Muni. Don't you?

(No response.)

BANTON: Sandy! You haven't heard a word I've said.

(He sits on the swing; she follows.)

PUTNAM: I'm sorry.

BANTON: What's wrong? You've been so quiet lately.

PUTNAM: I know.

BANTON: Is everything all right?

PUTNAM: My mind is wandering in all directions. I'm even getting careless at work. I missed a very important appointment today.

BANTON: What happened?

PUTNAM: I was on my way there, walking through the maternity ward—oh, forget it.

BANTON: Come on...what?

PUTNAM: It's embarrassing.

BANTON: Just say it.

PUTNAM: Well, I just stood there for I don't know how long looking at all the little babies. All I could think about was having a baby.

BANTON: That's embarrassing?

PUTNAM: I never thought about that before. That I could do that. Do you think about...?

BANTON: I suppose. Doesn't everyone think about that at one time or another?

PUTNAM: Not me. Not the people I spend time with! God, it can be so dull, analyzing, prognosticating, placing people in neat little categories—

BANTON: So why did you become a psychiatrist?

PUTNAM: I always wanted to be a doctor and psychiatry seemed so interesting. Well…I've never admitted this to anyone, and you must never tell a soul. *(She nods.)*

PUTNAM: I can't stand the sight of blood.

(They both laugh.)

PUTNAM: Is that ridiculous? I mean, I wanted to be a doctor, and I get nauseous if I get a paper cut!

BANTON: How did you ever get through medical school?

PUTNAM: Swiftly!

BANTON: You are funny, Sanford.

PUTNAM: I'm glad you appreciate my quick tongue. *(He realizes his mistake.)* Quick wit…

BANTON: *(Beat.)* Sandy. How were you in anatomy class?

PUTNAM: It wasn't one of my strongest subjects, if you know what I mean.

BANTON: I know what you mean.

PUTNAM: I know you know!

BANTON: There's no reason to be so nervous about all that.

PUTNAM: Do you believe that I'm my age, a top medical student, and I still don't know what I'm doing?

BANTON: It has nothing to do with knowledge.

PUTNAM: I'm not comfortable with you. Hell, I'm not comfortable with *me*! I don't like my body, and frankly, I don't like this conversation, so let's just drop it.

BANTON: I like your body.

PUTNAM: *(Skeptical.)* Really? What could you possibly see in me?

BANTON: Room for improvement?

(He gets annoyed and stands up. She goes to him.)

BANTON: That was a joke. Just relax.

PUTNAM: How do you "just relax"? I don't know how to do that.

(Banton signals him to come to her. He does, and she kisses him. He is too aggressive in return. She pulls away.)

PUTNAM: Now you've made me really self-conscious!

BANTON: Kiss me as gently as you possibly can. Hardly touch me.

(He takes a deep breath and he kisses her.)

BANTON: That was nice. You see. Everything is going to turn out just fine.

PUTNAM: When, and for how long?

(She laughs and takes him by the hand. They exit.)

Watbanalan

Doug Wright

Scene: Here and now
  1 Man and 1 Woman: Park (40) a man struggling to hold onto his marriag   (30s) his
  long-suffering wife.

Park is keeping a terrible secret from his wife. A year ago, he fathered a child with severe birth defects with his secretary and hasn't been able to have sex with Flo since that time. He has reluctantly agreed to accompany Flo to a marriage counselor, but when they arrive, he is barely able to keep his repressed guilty rage in check.

$$\bigcirc \qquad \bigcirc \qquad \bigcirc$$

(In front of them sits an invisible.)

PARK: What is this?

FLO: Shh. Honey.

PARK: Don't people write anymore? Don't people take notes?

FLO: Relax, Park.

PARK: Where do you store the tapes?

FLO: Really.

PARK: Are they secure? Are they kept confidential, under lock and key?

FLO: She broadcasts them every Sunday morning over the radio.

PARK: Can we keep the tapes?

FLO: Park…

PARK: I'd like to keep the tapes.

FLO: What for?

PARK: In a safe-deposit box.

FLO: Why don't you swallow them, whole, like a stolen key?

PARK: What I do with them doesn't matter. What matters is confiscation.

(Pause. Park and Flo lock eyes for a moment.)

FLO: Park would like you to know, Doctor, that he is not here of his own volition. I made our appointment. I drove the car. I put coinage in the meter.

PARK: Flo.

FLO: I pressed the appropriate floor.

PARK: I am here, aren't I? I am here today, this instant, right now. I am not coming here again. Understood?

(Pause. Flo abruptly turns to face the doctor, breaking the silence.)

73

...e were diligent. At first, we were persistent. Now our efforts
...ned.

PARK: Not entirely.

FLO: Now, Park...

PARK: Tell her, Flo. Our efforts have not altogether ceased.

(Flo is silent.)

PARK: Tell her.

FLO: I won't lie, Park.

(Pause.)

PARK: I see no reason, doctor...I see no reason to subject ourselves...our marriage...to routine disappointment. Not while the cause is a mystery. An
unknown. I fail, doctor, to understand our failure.

(Pause.)

FLO: Thirteen months.

PARK: Flo...

FLO: It has been thirteen months, two weeks and four days.

PARK: I can't will it to happen, Doctor. I can't flip a switch. It is not a *dog,* pant-
ing and wagging to please. Sit up, sit down, roll over. It doesn't respond to
commands.

FLO: It doesn't respond at all.

(Pause.)

PARK: The standard posture, tried and true.

FLO: I have done my best to encourage variations, doctor, but my suggestions
are routinely met with disdain, even...disgust.

PARK: The Kama Sutra is a fiction. The normal body, however fit, is incapable
of inverting itself so completely. Permuting itself beyond recognition. It is
foolish and inhibiting to shelve such books on our night table. The doctor,
I'm certain, will concur. Yes? *(Pause.)* No, I'm sorry. I can't envision myself
standing before some smarmy adolescent inquiring if *Lust Busters* is available for rental. Furthermore, doctor, I have seen enough to know such films
are anti-erotic. They are, in fact, medical. I would sooner watch brain
surgery. Shock therapy. Castration. *(Pause.)* Toys? Bobbing about on the bed
with rubber parts? Candy underclothes? Acting like babies in hopes of yield-
ing one? Don't insult us, doctor. *(Pause.) Don't sit smugly and prescribe. We
are not automatons. We are not broken clocks.*

FLO: Park—

PARK: *You don't know us. You don't know me.*

*(A long pause. Park fumes. Flo shifts ever so slightly in her seat. Finally, in a
small voice:)*

FLO: Do you want a child, Park?

74

PARK: I'm here. I'm trying.

FLO: Do you want my child?

PARK: What?

(Flo turns away.)

PARK: I'm doing the best I can.

(Pause. Flo looks imploringly at Park.)

PARK: Don't look at me. Don't stare. It doesn't help the situation. It doesn't exactly *move things along*.

FLO: I wish it were a tumor.

PARK: Don't.

FLO: I wish it were poison running through my body like blood. Then they could transfuse.

PARK: That's enough.

FLO: It's me, isn't it? It's what I am to you. *(Flo places her hand over her face. She begins to cry.)*

PARK: I want. I want so very much. If you could see inside my head. If you could know. Doctor. Help us. Help me. I'll try. I am trying, Flo.

FLO: Park?

PARK: Yes?

FLO: I love you?

(Park doesn't respond.)

PARK: *(Quietly:)* Help.

(Park and Flo don't move. Blackout.)

Watbanaland

Doug Wright

Scene: Here and now
    1 Man and 1 Woman: Park (40) a man struggling to hold onto his marriage and Flo (30s) his long-suffering wife.

Here, Flo tells Park of her desire for a child. Although he desperately needs to tell the truth about his illegitimate child, he cannot, and their conversation quickly devolves into a hurtful confrontation.

O   O   O

(The living room of the Stillman's apartment. Park sits at a small desk, with an open ledger. Flo needlepoints.)

PARK: How odd.

FLO: Hm?

PARK: These checks. There's no mention of these checks on the ledger.

FLO: I've been remiss.

PARK: When you write a check, make a note.

FLO: I apologize.

PARK: In the future—

FLO: Yes. In the future, I'll note each check. I'll deduct each total from the remaining balance listed on the pink line of the ledger. I'll write bold in legible script. Ink, never pencil. I'll perform these duties with the exactitude of a diamond cutter. *(Pause.)* Happy?

(Park stares at the checks.)

PARK: What is the Famine Fund?

FLO: It's my money, Park. I could spend it in worse ways. Some women buy oysters. Some buy satin sheets. Others, silk lingerie.

PARK: But not you.

FLO: No.

PARK: You buy children.

FLO: I do not *buy* children.

PARK: You rent children?

FLO: I *support* children.

PARK: If you're hell-bent on collecting babies, why waste time doing it through the mail? Just go outside and hail a cab. Drive up to the projects. Find an open window, and wait under it.

FLO: Not funny, Park.

(Park rifles through the checks.)

PARK: Sibdou, Burkina Faso. Maria, Ecuador. Moussi, Kenya. Jaime, Honduras. All yours?

FLO: They're mine, yes.

PARK: Is there a catalogue? An eight-hundred number?

FLO: Don't start, Park.

PARK: Late-night TV? That actress from the seventies. Coifed and grinning, glides through the dusty back roads of Sri Lanka, followed by a rainbow of children singing *"Kumbaya"* and proffering empty bowls...

FLO: Those children are starving.

PARK: How many, total?

FLO: Twenty-two.

PARK: That's going to take a mighty large shoe, Flo.

FLO: So be it. We're *well-heeled.*

(Flo smiles. She returns to her needlepoint. Park pauses, devises a new angle on the same subject.)

PARK: It's the worst kind of condescension.

FLO: Excuse me?

PARK: This *feel good* charity of yours. *(Park picks a check at random.)* "Baku, Watbanaland." You don't *know* this child. You don't know Africa. Oh to be fair, you've read a few *National Geographic's.* "How To Build a Quonset Hut." You've seen a few grainy photos in the *Times.* You've been to a Broadway show, with men in Kente cloth, harmonizing. You toss all these images into the Cuisinart that is your mind, add some sorry Polaroid of a bloated baby and—*voilà.* You white woman, have accepted your burden. Unto you a son is born. Perhaps—if one day, you actually meet this Baku—he will spit at your feet. Out of contempt for your ignorance. Your selfish appropriation.

FLO: What do we do, Park? Sit back, and atrophy in the face of our own shortcomings? No. It is our responsibility to do more.

PARK: *Our?* Oh, no. Not *our.* *(Park crosses to the bar and pours a drink.)* This is your project, not mine. I have hobbies of my own. Chess. Anagrams. This I leave to you.

FLO: Contrary to what your own experience might imply, the world is not some arid sphere. It's producing, all the time. Squeezing out life. It is incumbent upon us to nurture what the world spawns. *(Another brief rest.)* Like it or not, Park, it is our duty to perpetuate the species. *Ourselves.* In whatever way we can.

PARK: I disagree.

FLO: Oh?

PARK: Nature monitors herself. We should not intervene.

FLO: That's inhumane.

PARK: Starvation. Infanticide. Cannibalism. These are Nature's tools.

FLO: We have a function, Park. We play a role. Her conscience. We are here to enforce an ethical code.

PARK: When a dog whelps and a resulting pup is deficient—born with two heads, perhaps, or obstructed bowels—the bitch instinctively devours it. Her eyes dripping with maternal woe, she takes the newborn in her jaws and begins to chew. That is mercy in its purest form.

FLO: We are not animals. The same rules do not apply.

PARK: To allow it to live—muling across the floor, flopping to and fro—that is sadism. That, my dear, is moral bankruptcy.

FLO: You're being perverse.

PARK: We would do better, I think, if we had the courage…the strength of purpose…to eat our own.

(Park downs his drink. There is a long pause.)

FLO: I have not walked across burning sand, or watched my skin shrivel from lack of drink, but I have lived here in this desolate place, these eight sterile rooms, I have felt your cold, dry breath on my neck, and that is my own profound poverty.

I find solace in their pain. A sense of communion. In your parlance, a high return on my investment.

(Park tears up the canceled check slowly.)

PARK: I will not have our savings spent to mock me.

FLO: I beg your pardon?

PARK: The account bears my surname. I refuse to be party to my own humiliation.

FLO: That's preposterous.

PARK: Every decimal point trumpets my inadequacies. Every zero, an implied insult.

FLO: It's not about you.

PARK: It doesn't take a doctor, some smug Sigmund Freud, to recognize your rather puny attempts to compensate for my deficiencies.

FLO: You're over-reacting. This is nothing less than paranoia.

PARK: I'm closing the account.

FLO: But Park—

PARK: Likewise the subject.

Your Obituary Is A Dance
Benard Cummings

Scene: In Nella Rae's kitchen.
   Tommy (30s), effeminate and Nella Rae (30s) heavyset.

Tommy has just dropped in on an old friend, Nella Rae. He has AIDS, and lets on his time is almost up and asks for her help with his obituary.

○   ○   ○

NELLA: What's this for?

TOMMY: We gon' write my obituary together…

(Overlap dialogue.)

NELLA: …aw, hell, Tommy…un uh…naw…we'll have none of this…

TOMMY: …now wait a minute, Nella Rae…

NELLA: …here we is having a good time getting high, and me up in here on a roll preaching and all like I done lost my ever-loving mind…

TOMMY: …Nella Rae, hush and let me…

NELLA: …and here you is wanting to bring us all down with something crazy like this. I ain't gonna do no such thing. I don't like this—no way and no how…

(He stuffs a joint in her mouth.)

TOMMY: I don't like okra. But if I was starving I'd thank God for it and eat it. Now you listen to me: I am alive to do this. *Alive.* This way…we let go. Let go. *(Pause.)* C'mon my fat, black, nappy-headed, and beautiful Waitutsi woman. Me. You. And these words. *(He hands her the notebook. Pause.)* *(She finally takes it.)*

NELLA: I must be high to let you talk me into some simple shit like this. *(Pause.)* Well, don't be lookin' at me. What you wanna say here?

(Pause. They look at the paper like it's a foreign object.)

NELLA: Well, we can start by writing that "He was once a fierce drag queen…"

TOMMY: …un uh…don't you come for me. I never did that tired Patti LaBelle, Judy Garland thang. I personified performance art.

NELLA: Chile, please! You couldn't be Judy Garland even if you had Michael Jackson's money and plastic surgeon; and looka' here, I came to Dallas that time you was living there, and I saw that show you did at that cabaret. If that wasn't drag you was doing then I must've been blind, cripple and crazy.

TOMMY: Oh, girl, 'bye! I did lot's of confused things in those days 'fore I discovered that that wasn't my cup of tea.

NELLA: Cup?! You had a *pot!* Chile, who was it you was up there imitating?

TOMMY: …lip-synching…

NELLA: …whatever…

TOMMY: …Diana Ross!

NELLA: Yea! That was it! And you had the nerve to sing…

TOMMY: …lip-synch…

NELLA: …whatever…some "Sweetest Love Hangover!" Come here, Jesus!

TOMMY: Wasn't that a big ol' mess!

NELLA: You know, I used to love it when we were kids and you'd put on your Mu'dear's stuff and do me a little show.

TOMMY: You reaching waaaayyy back now.

NELLA: Remember that time she caught us up in ya'll's attic? Who was you imitating?

TOMMY: Donna Summer, girl.

NELLA: That's right! That's right! "Toot toot…ahhhh, beep beep. Bad girls, talkin' bout those bad girls…"

TOMMY: And the look on Mama's face when she caught us!

NELLA: Yeah! She looked like she didn't know whether to cry, faint, shit or holler. All she could do was do: "Tommy! agh ugh vvv rrr zzz what you doin? Stop that!" Miss sister-girl lost her mind.

TOMMY: Then she ran your little fat ass outta there…

NELLA: …un huh…accusing me of making you do that. As if she hadn't already noticed you was a big ol' sissy. Chile, please…

TOMMY: Did I ever tell you what happened after that?

NELLA: Naw, you never did.

TOMMY: Well, honey, she whipped me right out of that pageboy wig and them hot pants. Then she said that she just had to tell Papa so that he could put a stop to my foolishness. Well, Papa came into my room that night, mad as hell, and made Mama put that wig and hot pants on me. And some eye shadow. That's right, eye shadow. Chile, bye. Funny, Nella Rae, but the one clear thing I remember in that moment was that Mama was putting some ugly-ass dark purple eye shadow on me, and I was thinking that she had very little taste to be putting that dark-ass purple on my chocolate skin. But she was crying and shit, begging Papa not to make her do it. Now, Papa was never a violent man. Just as sweet as he could be. Didn't like me much, but a very sweet man. But he had this look in his eye like, Bitch, if you don't put it on him and r-a-t now, rat now, I'm gonna slap the taste out of you and this little sissy. Mama wasn't no fool: she put it on me. Then he made me start doing whatever it was I was doing up there in the attic. And, honey, he made that belt talk across my behind. All the while he kept saying that he was beating the deviance out of me. Truth is, I never hated him for that, Nella. I felt sorry for him. *(Pause.)* But in a lot of ways that whippin' prepared me well for life: if you think I caught hell from Black folks, white folks are truly another story.

NELLA: ...chile, say no more. *(Pause.)* So, now what do we put in this obituary?

TOMMY: Look, here it is: I have lived. I have learned. I have lost and won. Done cried. Done lied. And, yes, there were times when I witnessed the Truth. But no regrets 'cause now I rest. *(Pause.)* The end. *(Pause.)* Funny, but me and Papa will be buried side by side. Someday Mama will join us. And finally death will let us be together like life never could.

NELLA: Amen, baby. You is one sentimental bitch. Damn. *(She puts another tape into the jambox. Closes the notebook. Cheryl Lynn's "Got To Be Real" blasts from the speakers.)* Let's party, baby. Your obituary is a dance.

(They groove. Lights fade.)

Barking Sharks
Israel Horovitz

Scene: New York City, present
    2 Men: Ted (40s) Gloucester native fisherman and Eddie (40s), Gloucester native Advertising executive.

Eddie has returned to Gloucester after 25 years and has had an affair with Ted's wife Sara, his old girlfriend. He is disoriented by life. Here Eddie and Ted confront each other.

○   ○   ○

TED: I'll be fishin' Dabs, down East…It's not a huge stream. I could be back in like five days, if I get lucky. Gimme two more for the family, and then, I'm yours, Captain, *if* you can wait the extra week for me.
(Lights widen to include…Eddie, wearing foul-weather gear, boots.)
EDDIE: Sure, I can. No problem. I really appreciate this, Ted.
TED: Hey, what the hell…I'll probably make more crewin' for you, than I'll make runnin' my own pathetic tub. *(Holds up ripped net.)* Look'it this shit! We got rim-wracked, wicked, right off'a George's. I've only fished that same spot ten thousand times. You'd think I'd know what's down there!
EDDIE: It'll give us a chance to talk.
TED: What's that?
EDDIE: Nothing. I'm just thinking that going out fishing with you will give us a chance to talk.
TED: I hope not. I hope we're too busy hauling in some money. *(Throws net down.)* I've sewed this same hole so many times, there's none of the original net left! *(Looks up.)* It's tough, Eddie. You're gonna' see for yourself. I'm not bitchin'…I mean, I wouldn't trade places with nobody, but, it's tough, sometimes.
(Ted is upset. Eddie stares at him, a moment, before speaking.)
EDDIE: Ted, there are things you and I should be talking about…things that maybe shouldn't wait the week.
TED: Oh, yuh?…I guess I know like what.
EDDIE: You do?
TED: I talked to him for hours and hours, four days ago.
(Eddie stares at Ted, blankly, not comprehending. Ted explains.)
TED: Mac…about raggin' Little Eddie.
EDDIE: Oh. Right.
TED: He's just jealous, Eddie, that's all. Same as I was, when you first went off ta' college. When you're poor and you're staring at somebody who's not,

you feel kinda' stupid, really. You're askin' yourself "How come he's got this or that, when I've got nothin'?"…

EDDIE: I wasn't rich, growin' up. What are you saying?

TED: You are, now.

EDDIE: Yuh, but, Christ!…You can't imagine what I had to do for the money!

TED: That's kinda' my point. I can't. I can't imagine what it is you did. And if *I* can't, Mackie can't *begin* to! He just looks at Little Ed and thinks "It ain't fuckin' fair!"

EDDIE: He's probably right, too, 'cause, it ain't fuckin' fair. Only thing is, it's not Little Eddie's fault. I mean, whatever he is he is because I forced a kind of life on him. I did that.

TED: The way our parents did on us.

EDDIE: Exactly right. The way our parents did on us, and the way our kids will on their kids.

TED: Sara's wick'id happy you're back in town, Ed.

EDDIE: I'm…glad.

TED: I myself am glad you're back, too, Eddie. It worried me, at first…I went through a lot'ta personal bullshit, but, no more…Seeing you, being with you…it makes me feel, I dunno…*younger. (Beat.)* Eddie?

EDDIE: What?

TED: I know about the other stuff, too.

EDDIE: You do?

TED: I do. Thanks for not sayin' "What other stuff?"

EDDIE: What other stuff?

TED: Fuck you.

EDDIE: I don't know where to begin, Teddy, except to say it's totally over. Both of us feel terrible, and it's over.

TED: I'm glad to hear that.

EDDIE: I take responsibility for my part in it. It was wrong. We were both wrong. We knew it, right away. We were both pretending it was twenty-five years ago. It was crazy. I mean, it wasn't like Sara was falling out of love with you and back into love with me…believe me! It was nothing like that! It was like we were kids again, and, finally, ending it *properly.* Have you and Sara talked?

TED: On this?…No. There's a big part of me that wants to beat the living shit out of you.

EDDIE: There's a big part of me that *wants* you to beat the living shit out of me!

TED: Anybody else, he'd be a dead man!

EDDIE: I know this, Ted.

TED: It's so fucked up! I'd be out on my boat, just knowin' the two of ya's were together. It was eatin' me up. I'd be havin' these thoughts, like she was still really yours, and I, like, don't deserve her 'cause she was yours and I like took her from you, behind your back…*(Suddenly.)* Jesus, Eddie, she's my *wife!* How could you go off with my *wife?!*

(Ted punches Eddie, twice, bloodying Eddie's lip. Eddie doesn't defend himself. He takes both blows, staggers backward, face unprotected. Ted is about to throw the killer punch…but he doesn't. He stops himself.)

TED: You okay?

EDDIE: Yuh, I guess. Feel any better?

TED: Not much. *(Beat.)* Yuh, I guess I do, a little. Thanks.

EDDIE: I'm so sorry, Ted.

TED: I guess you probably are. *(Beat.)* Never again means never again, right?

EDDIE: On the love of my son, I swear this to you, Ted.

TED: I want to never talk on this, again.

EDDIE: Agreed.

TED: If you go back on your word…if you touch my wife, again…you're a dead man.

EDDIE: I never will. I love you, man.

TED: Fuck you. *(Beat.)* Eddie?

(Eddie looks up. Ted tosses him a clean handkerchief to wipe his bloody lip. And then…)

TED: Vinnie Santo screwed you. His boat's a piece of shit! Sixty-six thousand was a crazy price. *(Starts toward net to leave.)*

EDDIE: Ted, I…Please, don't leave!…Ted, please, listen to me…There was a Soviet cosmonaut who was up in space for months and months. When he came back down to Earth, he expected to be some kind of hero. But, two days before he landed, the Soviet Union dissolved. There was practically nobody waiting for him. And he could not begin to understand what had happened!…When I left Gloucester, it was possible to have some kind of authentic life here. I went away and I came back, but, where's the Gloucester I left? Where is the Earth for me to put my feet on? Why am I here, Ted? Every move I've made in my entire life has been a mistake…leaving here…coming back…betraying my family…betraying you…Who am I, Ted? *I don't know who I am!*…Don't hate me, Ted. Please.

TED: I don't hate you, Eddie. I feel sorry for you. *(Beat. Picks up net.)* I've gotta' go, Eddie. I've got a trip.

Below the Belt

Richard Dresser

Scene: Company's living quarters
    2 Men: Hanrahan, a man and Dobbitt, the new worker.

Dobbitt arrives at Hanrahan's living quarters and they speak.

O   O   O

(In darkness we hear Hanrahan attempting to type. He responds to each key-stroke, which echoes in the silent room.)
HANRAHAN: Excellent. *(Another keystroke.)* Good. Very good. *(Five quick key-strokes.)* Beautiful. *Beautiful.* Keep it up. Nice and steady. *(Three quick ones.)* Damn you! Damn you to hell! Bastard! *(The sound of paper being viciously crumpled and another piece of paper being put in the typewriter. A pause, then a hesitant keystroke.)* Okay, all right, that's the idea. Easy does it.
(The lights slowly come up on Hanrahan's room, which is small and makeshift, with two small beds, a simple cooking arrangement, an old radio, and a door to the bathroom. Hanrahan is laboriously typing at a desk with a large, old-fashioned typewriter. Dobbitt enters, carrying a suitcase. He stands there a moment, not wanting to interrupt. Hanrahan doesn't acknowledge him.)
DOBBITT: I'm Dobbitt. *(Pause, then louder.)* I'm Dobbitt.
HANRAHAN: *(Not looking up.)* Can't you wait 'til I'm done?
(Hanrahan stares at the typewriter. Dobbitt puts his suitcase down as quietly as possible, barely making a sound. Hanrahan turns and glares at him.)
HANRAHAN: What's all this ruckus? I'm busy. I'm looking for the "y."
(Dobbitt goes over and hits the "y" on the typewriter which makes a loud echoing sound. Hanrahan stares at Dobbitt.)
HANRAHAN: Well, well, well. Very impressive. He knows just where they keep the "y." *(Hanrahan stands up, takes the paper from the typewriter, puts it in an envelope, seals the envelope, puts the envelope in a manila folder, puts the folder in a large envelope which he seals, then puts the large envelope in a drawer, which he locks. He puts the key in his pocket, which he buttons.)*
DOBBITT: I was just trying to help.
HANRAHAN: I don't like people looking over my shoulder, passing judgment. There's going to be trouble if you pry into my affairs. Who are you, anyway?

DOBBITT: I'm Dobbitt. You must be Hanrahan.

HANRAHAN: I *must* be Hanrahan? I don't have a choice?

DOBBITT: Are you Hanrahan?

HANRAHAN: Who are you to barge into my room and tell me who I must be?

DOBBITT: You're not Hanrahan?

HANRAHAN: As it turns out, I *am* Hanrahan, but not because it happens to suit your purposes.

DOBBITT: I'm sorry. It was an endless flight and then we drove for hours through the desert. This is where they told me to stay.

HANRAHAN: You're staying here? In my room?

DOBBITT: It's a two-person room. They told me there was someone in here before.

HANRAHAN: Haney. He left early.

DOBBITT: Why did he leave? Did something happen?

HANRAHAN: (A long look at Dobbitt.) Which bed?

DOBBITT: Oh, it doesn't matter.

HANRAHAN: Yes it does. This one in the corner gets an icy wind off the desert snapping right through it. The window doesn't close. A man could freeze to death in this bed.

DOBBITT: If it's all the same to you, I'll take the other bed.

HANRAHAN: Suit yourself.

(Dobbitt throws his suitcase down on the bed and starts unpacking. Hanrahan pours himself a mug of coffee.)

HANRAHAN: That one's a sweat box. Right next to the radiator, which clangs in your ear like a train wreck all night long. You'll be begging for mercy by morning.

DOBBITT: Why don't we move the beds?

HANRAHAN: That's an idea. That should solve everything.

(Dobbitt tries to move the bed.)

HANRAHAN: Except they're bolted to the floor. Lots of thievery on the compound.

DOBBITT: They're stealing beds?

HANRAHAN: Not since the bolts went in.

DOBBITT: Which bed do you sleep in?

HANRAHAN: Both. I start in the one next to the window. When I start to freeze I climb in the other one. Then, when I can't breathe I get up and start the day. I guess that's all gone now that *you're* here.

DOBBITT: I seem to have caught you at a bad time.

HANRAHAN: Oh?

DOBBITT: I fear I've upset you.

HANRAHAN: *You've* upset me? That's a bit grandiose, don't you think?

DOBBITT: You seem disgruntled.

HANRAHAN: Gruntled or disgruntled, it has nothing to do with you.

(Dobbitt watches Hanrahan sipping from a cup. He yawns.)

DOBBITT: Is that coffee?

HANRAHAN: Yes. *(Hanrahan doesn't move.)*

DOBBITT: I feel as though I've been traveling forever. I should either sleep or try to revive myself. If there's any more coffee.

HANRAHAN: There's plenty more coffee. *(Hanrahan still doesn't move.)*

DOBBITT: I could get it myself.

HANRAHAN: Are you asking for coffee?

DOBBITT: Only if it's no bother.

HANRAHAN: Well of course it's a bother! *(Hanrahan angrily starts clattering around the coffeepot.)*

DOBBITT: Then please, forget it.

HANRAHAN: Now that I'm knee-deep in it you don't want any?

DOBBITT: If it's easier to continue…

HANRAHAN: *(Turning on him.)* See here. I'm not a puppet on a string. You'll have to make up your mind and you'll have to do it right now.

DOBBITT: No coffee. I don't want to put you out.

HANRAHAN: I'm already put out. The only question is whether or not you want coffee.

DOBBITT: Everything else being equal, I would say yes to coffee.

HANRAHAN: Very well. *(He pours a cup of coffee.)* It just means I have to make a whole new pot for myself.

(He hands it to Dobbitt who tries to refuse the coffee.)

DOBBITT: Then you take this, please—

HANRAHAN: No!

DOBBITT: I insist!

(As they struggle, the coffee spills on Hanrahan, who bellows.)

DOBBITT: My God! I'm terribly sorry—

HANRAHAN: Look what you've done!

DOBBITT: It was an accident—

HANRAHAN: If you'd made up your mind this never would have happened. *(Hanrahan dries himself with a towel. There's a beep from a small intercom on the wall. Hanrahan stops and glares at it.)* Well. That's Merkin. And he sounds upset. *(Grimly.)* Come on, Dobbitt, it's time to meet the boss.

Below the Belt

Richard Dresser

Scene: An office
   3 Men: Hanrahan, the new worker, Dobbitt, a man and Merkin, their boss.

Dobbitt has just arrived at an industrial compound in a distant land. He has met his roommate and co-worker, Hanrahan, and now meets his boss, Merkin.

O   O   O

(Lights up on Merkin's office, which contains a desk, a desk chair, and one other chair, which looks none too comfortable. A window with drawn blinds looks out on the compound. Merkin peers out through the blinds. Dobbitt and Hanrahan enter. Dobbitt comes forward and shakes hands with Merkin.)

MERKIN: Welcome, Dobbitt. I'm Merkin.

DOBBITT: I'm thrilled to be here, Merkin.

MERKIN: Thrilled? That seems a bit extreme.

DOBBITT: It's my very first off-country assignment. I've had extensive experience in-country, however—

MERKIN: Yes, yes, we've read your file. We frankly know more about your life than we'd like. Make yourself comfortable.

(Hanrahan quickly sits in the one chair. Merkin sits at his desk. Dobbitt looks in vain for another chair, then assumes what he hopes is a casual stance.)

MERKIN: We're in a fix and there's no time to waste. On November fifth we're delivering the largest order this company has ever received. The work must be meticulously checked if we're to avoid penalties and crippling lawsuits and a tarnished reputation that could bring the corporation to its knees. Unfortunately, until this moment, we've been short one Checker.

DOBBITT: What happened to the last Checker?

MERKIN: Why don't you ask your friend Hanrahan?

DOBBITT: *(Turning to Hanrahan.)* Well?

HANRAHAN: He's no friend of mine.

MERKIN: It's enough to say we need you, Dobbitt. You come highly recommended.

DOBBITT: My assignments have been serendipitous to date, and I have no reason to believe this will be any different.

(A sudden laugh from Hanrahan. Dobbitt turns but Hanrahan is staring at the floor.)

MERKIN: All three plants are operational twenty-four hours a day. You'll tour the compound and see. We turn out seven thousand one hundred and eighty-six units per eight-hour shift. Which means with all three shifts we do—

HANRAHAN: Twenty-one thousand five hundred and fifty-eight units a day.

MERKIN: So over a six-day work week we do—

HANRAHAN: One hundred twenty-nine thousand three hundred and forty-eight units.

MERKIN: Factor in a loss of 3 percent based on our checking—feel free to jump in, Dobbitt.

DOBBITT: Uh, let's see…I'm just so tired from my trip…

HANRAHAN: Twenty thousand nine hundred and eleven units a day, one hundred twenty-five thousand four hundred and sixty-six units per week.

MERKIN: Thank you. I'm glad *someone* is paying attention. Our delivery date is November fifth, which means at our current rate when will we be done? Dobbitt?

DOBBITT: Oh…I think we'll make it in plenty of time.

HANRAHAN: We'll finish November third at 10:30 P.M.

MERKIN: Why do I have November second?

HANRAHAN: Aren't you forgetting the holiday?

MERKIN: Quite right, quite right. Human error. In any event, we have a gun aimed at our head and without a system our brains will be trickling down the wall when November rolls around. While Hanrahan is out checking, Dobbitt will be typing his reports. While Dobbitt is out checking, Hanrahan will be typing his reports. Any questions?

DOBBITT: It sounds like a perfect arrangement.

MERKIN: That's not a question. This is where you're allowed to ask questions.

DOBBITT: I have none. Thank you.

MERKIN: No questions?

DOBBITT: Most people would have a question here?

MERKIN: Frankly, I'm surprised.

DOBBITT: All right, all right…my question—

MERKIN: Don't ask a question just for the sake of asking a question. Ask only if you want to know the answer.

DOBBITT: I'm fine with no questions.

MERKIN: On the other hand, there's no such thing as a stupid question.

DOBBITT: Tell me, what exactly are those units you spoke of?

MERKIN: Pardon me?

DOBBITT: The units would be…what? What are we making in these factories?

MERKIN: Hear that, Hanrahan?

(Merkin and Hanrahan laugh.)

DOBBITT: I'm just very—

MERKIN: We're well aware of how tired you are. I'd like the two of you to function as a team. Personalities—such as they are in this case—rank a distant second.

DOBBITT: That's my philosophy. I'll do anything I can for the team. While I may not be quite as quick with figures as some, I'm an excellent typist.

MERKIN: Which is to say?

DOBBITT: It might speed things up if Hanrahan helped me with the calculations and I pitched in on his typing.

HANRAHAN: That's not necessary, Dobbitt.

DOBBITT: I just meant in the heat of battle—

HANRAHAN: I said it's not necessary, Dobbitt!

MERKIN: Hanrahan, you're free to go on your merry way. I'd like to tell Dobbitt how we do things on the compound.

(Hanrahan gets up to leave.)

DOBBITT: Thanks, Hanrahan.

HANRAHAN: *(Turning on him.)* For what? For what, Dobbitt?

MERKIN: All right, Hanrahan, that's enough.

HANRAHAN: I demand to know why Dobbitt is thanking me.

MERKIN: Dobbitt, why are you thanking Hanrahan?

DOBBITT: For welcoming me to the compound.

HANRAHAN: I never did that.

DOBBITT: For sharing your room.

HANRAHAN: I did it under duress.

DOBBITT: For what I just know will be a wonderful partnership.

HANRAHAN: If the platitudes have abated, I'll take my leave.

(Hanrahan leaves. Merkin gives Dobbitt a long look.)

MERKIN: So. What has Hanrahan said about me?

DOBBITT: Nothing at all.

MERKIN: I'm not worthy of mention?

DOBBITT: He *mentioned* you. There hasn't been time for more than that.

MERKIN: Does he hate me?

DOBBITT: Please! Of course not!

MERKIN: How do you know?

DOBBITT: To be honest, I don't *know*.

MERKIN: Then there's a possibility he hates me?

DOBBITT: I am completely unfamiliar with the situation, and after all that time in the air—

MERKIN: I've heard all I can stomach about your damnable flight!

DOBBITT: Well…I suppose technically there's a possibility…

MERKIN: Of what?

DOBBITT: That Hanrahan…

MERKIN: What?

DOBBITT: Hates you.

MERKIN: Dear God.

DOBBITT: Although I have no reason to believe it's true.

MERKIN: If you have no reason to believe it's true then why do you dangle it in front of me, like some terrible carcass rotting on a meat hook? Why, Dobbitt, why?

DOBBITT: I...I don't know...

MERKIN: There's something you should know. Hanrahan and I have served here together for nearly one year. In that time we have grown to be close friends. I trust you'll respect that.

DOBBITT: Of course. No harm was intended.

MERKIN: It never is. Do you know, I am responsible for everything that happens in this entire department? It's a lonely and treacherous job. *(He gets a large, imposing stamp from a desk drawer.)* I make the hard decisions. The people decisions. Who goes up, who goes down. And who stays locked in place, shackled in bureaucratic leg irons until all hope is lost. *(Merkin slams the stamp on a piece of paper. It echoes ominously. He turns the paper to Dobbitt.)* What does that say?

DOBBITT: "Void."

MERKIN: Exactly. I expect we'll get along fine, Dobbitt.

(Merkin starts going through papers. Dobbitt is unsure what to do.)

DOBBITT: Am I...dismissed?

MERKIN: You may come and go as you please. You're a highly skilled professional and that's exactly how you'll be treated.

DOBBITT: Thank you. *(Dobbitt starts for the door.)*

MERKIN: Oh, Dobbitt? Entre nous, I'd be careful, razzing old Hanrahan about his typing.

DOBBITT: I wasn't razzing!

MERKIN: Sounded like razzing to me. You razzed him up and down and back and forth. You're quite the razzer, Dobbitt.

DOBBITT: I'm no razzer! I wouldn't know how to razz!

MERKIN: He's damned sensitive about his typing. Hell, you might as well have razzed him about his *dancing*. I'd hate to have you discover that the hard way. Consider yourself dismissed.

(Lights fade as Dobbitt leaves.)

Clean

Edwin Sanchez

Scene: a church
    2 Men: Gustavito (18) a young man trying to reconcile his love for a priest, and Father (30s) the man he loves.

Gustavito has been in love with Father ever since he was a little boy. After several years apart, Gustavito returns to the church to make a final confession.

○   ○   ○

(Gustavito enters church. He walks around slowly, Father enters.)
FATHER: We're not opened right now.
GUSTAVITO: Hey Father.
(Father stares at him for a moment.)
GUSTAVITO: Back from the dead, so to speak.
FATHER: Gustavito.
GUSTAVITO: Have I changed a lot? What do you think Father?
FATHER: When did you get back?
GUSTAVITO: I came back for my mother's funeral. Not Mercy, Esperanza. My *real* mother. I haven't seen her yet. They could put any corpse in front of me and I would be expected to cry on cue.
FATHER: Whatever happened, Gustavito, she was your mother.
GUSTAVITO: Yes, Father, she was. Hey, it was an excuse to come back. I'm all cured now.
FATHER: I didn't know you were sick.
GUSTAVITO: You were the cause.
(Father looks down.)
GUSTAVITO: First love, worse love.
FATHER: Gustavito.
GUSTAVITO: Gustavo.
FATHER: Gustavo. You're a young man now.
GUSTAVITO: Fifteen. You wanna sit?
(Father and Gustavito sit on a pew.)
FATHER: How's your family?
GUSTAVITO: Everybody's fine. Real happy, like always.
FATHER: Good. Does God still talk to you?
GUSTAVITO: I talk to Him.

92

FATHER: Does He listen?

GUSTAVITO: I'm here, aren't I? *(Pause.)* So who replaced me? Who became your altar boy?

FATHER: Domingo.

(Gustavito laughs.)

GUSTAVITO: I knew it. Little prick. Excuse me. Before I left I was going to kill him. Seriously. Well, as seriously as a ten-year-old can think of something like that.

FATHER: As I recall you were a very serious ten-year-old.

GUSTAVITO: I didn't think you had any memory of me. So, first I was going to kill him then I decided it should be you. And me. I can't believe I'm confessing out here. Can we go to the confessional?

FATHER: This is fine.

(Gustavito rises.)

GUSTAVITO: Please.

(Father enters his space and Gustavito enters his.)

GUSTAVITO: Forgive me Father for I have sinned. It has been five years since my last confession.

FATHER: Go ahead.

GUSTAVITO: You used to say, "Go ahead, my son."

FATHER: Go ahead, my son.

GUSTAVITO: So, you glad to see me?

(Silence.)

GUSTAVITO: Okay, where did I leave off? Oh yeah, I was going to kill us. I started hating you and me and I figured the pain would be better than the hate. But I didn't, so. Does that count as a sin? I thought it, but I didn't do it.

FATHER: Do you repent?

GUSTAVITO: I can't. Anyway, I don't have to. I'm over it. You.

FATHER: That's good.

GUSTAVITO: It's different for you. You never had anything to get over, right?

FATHER: You know, I could never find my rosary after you left.

GUSTAVITO: That's a shame. This little box was the safest place in the world to me. Where I first heard your voice, you remember?

FATHER: I really should get back.

GUSTAVITO: To what? I am over you.

(Father tries to leave the confessional, Gustavito grabs his wrist.)

GUSTAVITO: I am over you.

FATHER: I understand.

(Gustavito slowly lets go of Father's wrist.)

GUSTAVITO: Gotta go. Oh, my penance.

FATHER: Please don't come here again.

GUSTAVITO: That ought to do it. *(Gustavito reaches into his pocket and pulls out the Father's rosary.)* I was saving it for you. Here.

(Father does not move. Gustavito dangles the rosary.)

GUSTAVITO: Take it.

(Father does.)

GUSTAVITO: I wasn't going to keep it from you. It's yours. What's the Latin word for impossible? Never mind. I'm over you.

(Gustavito exits. Father kneels, holding the rosary. He places it around his neck and slowly fingers the beads.)

FATHER: I've missed you.

Emma's Child

Kristine Thatcher

Scene: In the woods, in the rain
    2 Men: Sam and Henry.

Sam and Henry discuss roughing it, as it applies to the relationships with the women in their lives.

O   O   O

SAM: Birch bark, that's what we need.
(He attempts to light another wet match. Henry looks on with a mixture of thinly veiled pity and contempt.)
HENRY: What's that you say?
SAM: We could get this fire going if we had birch bark. In a wet woods, you can always start a fire with birch bark. The Indians used it for everything. You can write letters on it. You can sew with it, lace up your moccasins with it. You can even build a canoe. The bark has petroleum in its skin, which makes it not only waterproof, but also flammable. It's a natural accelerant.
HENRY: That's wonderful.
SAM: Oh, yeah. Find yourself a piece of drenched birch bark, set a match to it, and you've got yourself a fire.
HENRY: It's white, isn't it, Sam? Birch bark?
SAM: That's right.
HENRY: Is that a birch over there? *(Indicating something in the distance.)*
SAM: *(Sam looks up.)* Yes, it is. That's a yellow birch. The Irish considered that particular kind of birch to be a bewitching tree. I think they called it the white lady of death. They actually believed the top branches could reach down and touch your soul. If it did that, you were a goner.
HENRY: Lots of birch bark right there, then.
SAM: That's a live tree, Henry. We'll pay a five hundred dollar fine if they catch us messing with a live tree. A birch is fragile; if it has open places in the skin, the insects get inside and kill it.
HENRY: Oh.
SAM: The wind plays havoc with it, too.
HENRY: Too bad.
SAM: But, even if that *was* a dead tree?
HENRY: Yeah?

SAM: We've got a helluva a lot of soggy matches here. Birch bark doesn't ignite all by itself.

HENRY: So, the subject of birch bark is pretty much a moot one.

SAM: Pretty moot. A doggone waste of breath, actually. Now, if I'd thought to bring along some steel wool, we could unravel a piece of it, and together with the flashlight batteries, get a spark going.

HENRY: But, you didn't think to bring steel wool?

SAM: No, I didn't. Even if I had, we'd still need a heck of a lot of—

TOGETHER: Birch bark.

SAM: It's your basic Catch-22.

(Indicating bottle of vodka that Henry clutches to his side.)

SAM: Don't bogey that bottle.

HENRY: *(Surrendering it.)* I'm going to remember what I've learned tonight. You never know when you'll get yourself stuck in the middle of a wet woods, in freezing weather, with night coming on.

SAM: It's handy information.

HENRY: It is. *(Beat.)* However, strictly speaking, a Catch-22 it is not, Sam. If you're in the mood to split hairs, and what the fuck else do we have to do on a night like this? A Catch-22 is a situation where something desirable is unattainable because one of its requirements can never exist in the presence of some other of its requirements.

SAM: Say again?

HENRY: The lack of fire-making tools is only really a Catch-22, if the necessary birch bark isn't available precisely because steel wool is, or vice versa.

SAM: Ah. I see. *(Silence.)* Would the term *snafu* be more applicable?

HENRY: I believe I can allow it, yes.

SAM: Fine. Tell me this—

HENRY: Yes?

SAM: Jean puts up with you every day and every night, is that right?

HENRY: Essentially.

SAM: Wonderful woman.

HENRY: Patient woman, yes. Might I add that it is my sincere hope that the tranquillity of your marriage to Franny did not rest on your fire-building abilities.

SAM: It did not.

HENRY: Good.

SAM: Goddamn Mount Pinatubo. It'll warm up tomorrow. But, hell, if it's warm, if it's cold, if we freeze our butts off, I'll still take the woods every time. I can finally breathe! Can you breathe?

HENRY: No problem so far.

SAM: How I ever came to believe a transfer to the New York office of Arthur Anderson was my destiny calling, I will never know. Anyway, my kid is married, my wife has fled the scene, and I am thinking about coming back here for good.

HENRY: Back to Michigan? What would you do?

SAM: Start my own accounting firm. I was raised in the woods.

HENRY: No kidding?

SAM: Hell, yes. My folks owned a lodge in Gaylord. This is home to me. I've come home! God! I love it here. There's no duplicity here. There's no room for liars here. You've gotta tough it out, know what I mean?

HENRY: Not exactly, Sam. My definition of roughing it has always involved a screen door of some kind.

SAM: You've never been camping?

HENRY: Hotels and boardwalks come strongly into play when I'm defining a really swell vacation. Give me white sand, a mai tai, and some sun tan oil, and I am on vacation!

SAM: Why did you suggest camping, then?

HENRY: Was this my idea?

SAM: If memory serves.

HENRY: You're kidding! I don't know. I thought I could get you to meet me here. I know you like to camp.

SAM: Well, next time suggest the mai tai, sun tan oil thing.

HENRY: You got it.

SAM: *(He shakes his head. Humiliated.)* It's the kindness that's killing me. All the mushroom soup and tuna casseroles from neighbor ladies, the endless analysis over drinks with well-meaning pals, and now this: Deliverance 2.

HENRY: It wasn't just for you. I needed to get away.

SAM: Yeah?

HENRY: Yeah.

SAM: I heard you guys are in trouble.

HENRY: It's a mess.

SAM: She really wants to bring that kid home?

HENRY: She really does.

SAM: If she does, then what? Will you leave?

HENRY: She wouldn't. She won't.

SAM: There's no telling what a woman will do, especially one who knows she's suckered your trust. You're a writer.

HENRY: Sometimes.

SAM: Then you know about the weakness in human nature. Women are the worst. Tell me about Franny, for example.

HENRY: I beg your pardon?

SAM: Quote somebody. Tell me I'm not crazy. Tell me the worst thing anybody ever wrote about a woman.

HENRY: Why would you want—?

SAM: Or women, in general. Let's throw caution to the wind, and just lump 'em all together, what do you say? Because, after seventeen years, I never thought I could hate her, but I do.

HENRY: Hate?

SAM: I financed that fucking birthing center of hers. It was the biggest mistake of my life. Once it took off, we were stuck. There was no considering a transfer out of that hell hole. She was in paradise. She was always so—lah-de-dah, off to the theatre, galleries in Soho, concerts in Central Park. "Let's step over this inert body to get a better view of the Chrysler Building." Jesus Christ, if I'd had to hear her wax sentimental one more time about the fucking Chrysler building—have you been to New York lately?

HENRY: What are you talking about?

SAM: Calcutta without the cows, that's what I'm talking about. Mass psychosis! I can hardly leave the house any more. From an airplane, it looks exactly like a malignant skin tumor.

HENRY: But I thought—

SAM: After all the years I suffocated in that pit for her sake, I lose my mind when I think of her with that jerk—I think up tortures. I dream of murder.

HENRY: Whoa.

SAM: If one other person has hated a woman the way I hate Franny, I might survive. So tell me the worst. It was probably Shakespeare, wasn't it? Shakespeare could hate a woman, couldn't he?

HENRY: What?

SAM: Shakespeare could hate a woman.

HENRY: Yes.

SAM: Couldn't he?

HENRY: He could be venomous on the subject, yes.

SAM: What'd he say? Hit me with it! No holds barred!

HENRY: That's good. "No holds Bard." I like that.

SAM: Go ahead.

HENRY: Let me think. Well, there's *King Lear: (Scanning beautifully.)* Behold yon simp'ring dame,

Something, something

Down from the waist they are something,

Something, something

But to the waist do the gods inherit,

Beneath is all the fiend's.
There's hell, there's darkness, there is the sulphurous pit,
Burning scalding, something, something; fie, fie, fie!
SAM: *(Who has stopped carefully laying matches to dry on a towel, in order that he may listen:)* "The sulphurous pit?" He actually said that?
HENRY: Takes your breath away, doesn't it?
SAM: That's some memory you got there. Something, something.
HENRY: Does that do it for you?
SAM: It comes pretty damn close. Doesn't *quite* say it, but it comes close.
HENRY: Then there's Yeats, who wrote about forgiveness.
SAM: Fuck him.
HENRY: Right.

The Professional
Dusan Kovacevic

Translated and adapted by Bob Djurdjevic

Scene: a rundown publishing house in Eastern Europe
>   2 Men: Theodore "Teya" Kry (45) once a dissident intellectual, now a publisher and Luke
>   Laban (60s) a retired policeman.

>   *Luke's professional career was spent managing the round-the clock surveillance of Teya, a man
>   once considered to be a dangerous enemy of the state. Luke's observation soon turned to
>   obsession as he saw in Teya's speeches a key to understanding his own son, a college profes-
>   sor. Prompted by his son, Luke managed to capture all of Teya's speeches and stories on paper,
>   and bound them into several handsome volumes. When his son escapes to the West and com-
>   munism falls, Luke finds himself out of a job and very lonely. He finally makes a visit to Teya
>   with the intention of making a gift of the volumes that represent nearly two decades of work.
>   Here, the two adversaries reveal their basic differences.*

TEYA: How long have you been a taxi driver?

LUKE: Since your gang came to power.

TEYA: My gang?

LUKE: That's right. You heard me.

TEYA: What do you mean my *gang,* Comrade Luke?

LUKE: I mean the ones that are in government now. The new ones. The intel-
ligent and infallible ones. If only I knew how they manage to keep themselves free from sin. Maybe they're foreigners?

TEYA: But what have I got to do with them?

LUKE: I don't know. I really don't know. I'm no longer in the service, so I'm
not very well informed.

TEYA: Then who gave you the right to link me with them?

LUKE: Who gave me the right? You ask me who gave me the right?

TEYA: Yes, Comrade Luke. I ask you who gave you that right?

LUKE: No one has ever given me anything, Teya. They only grab and take from
me. They took away my job, my honor, my self-respect, my health, and my
son. They took away everything I gained in thirty years of servitude.

TEYA: If you wanted to insult me, you picked the worst possible way. You're
speaking like those fools in there. *(Teya points to the wall of the adjacent
office where the music continues to come from.)* Why do you think my *gang*
threw you out?

LUKE: Because, Teya, you have been an enemy of this country for twenty years. Then, once again overnight—because in this country everything happens overnight—I turn out to be the enemy and they appoint you to this job. Me the taxi driver, you a director. Me on the street, you in a plush office.

TEYA: Comrade Luke, I don't know any of the people in power today. I have nothing to do with them whatsoever!

LUKE: Maybe you think you have nothing to do with them, but they have a lot to do with you. You think that you got this job without their knowledge and consent? Do you think you were given this job because you deserved it? Is that what you think?

TEYA: Yes. That's exactly what I think, Comrade Luke. I think that I deserve this job. Certainly more than the locksmiths, plumbers, sheet-metal workers and other Bolshevik intellectuals who got their doctorates after two years of trade school. We make books here, not nails, horseshoes, or metal joints!

LUKE: Naturally, I agree. But, what interests me, Teya, is how you suddenly come to believe that now someone can get a position that they deserve and are qualified for, when only yesterday you claimed that the entire Bolshevik system rested exclusively on blind subservience and loyalty, and not on the basis of knowledge or intelligence. What makes you think that you are suddenly an exception, when you know that they are in complete control, that they pay attention to every detail and that there are no exceptions. None, Teya, my son!

TEYA: I know that, but...

LUKE: There is no "but," my friend! No "but!" After thirty years of working for them, I am telling you there is no "but." Only "either-or!" Either you're theirs, whatever you might think, or you're not, in which case you're nothing, you just don't exist. You were brought here...

TEYA: May I please ask you not to use your charming police expressions, "brought" and "taken away" in this room. This is not a police station. And if it is of any interest to you, people begged me to come here, to get rid of the dogs who ran this place, and to try to save this publishing house from liquidation. Of course, that's impossible, but I will still try, because this publishing house has two hundred employees...

LUKE: A hundred and fifty-six.

TEYA: A hundred and fifty-six?

LUKE: A hundred and fifty-six.

TEYA: They told me two hundred.

LUKE: A hundred and fifty-six.

TEYA: All right, a hundred and fifty-six employees and as many families who were driven to the edge of starvation by this bunch of thieves and cutthroats. Only a madman would have accepted this job, because there's no hope for any of us until the whole system is changed. I know that better than you, because I have experienced it myself. Words and books can do nothing against the army and the police. And if indeed somebody "brought" me here, as you claim, if somebody authorized my coming here, if somebody asked somebody else, and if somebody told somebody to tell somebody that it was all okay, than that somebody did that so I would destroy myself with great fanfare and finally bring this publishing house down with me! I know all that very well, Comrade Luke, but I am a bit surprised that you don't understand why they fired you, why they…

LUKE: Drove me away, "like peasants driving away an old dog that can no longer run, bark or bite?", if you will allow me to quote you.

TEYA: I didn't say that. If that's what you thought, then that's your problem.

LUKE: You said it.

TEYA: When did I say it?

LUKE: The day when my son said it to me—quoting what you said about your own father.

TEYA: That's not true, Comrade Luke! That's not true!

LUKE: Speak softer so I can hear you.

TEYA: The last time I had a fight with my father, I told him that he and his generation had served people who were worse than themselves. That they fought against injustice—for injustice; against evil—for an even greater evil; against fictitious enemies—for real existing enemies!

LUKE: I know, I know all that.

TEYA: I told him all that, but I never mentioned the "peasant's dog."

LUKE: You described how the peasants took the worn-out dog into the forest, and killed it there out of kindness, far from the house it had guarded, far from the family and children who had learned to walk hanging onto his fur. In the evening, on the same leash, they return with a new dog that will serve them until it is time to go to the forest again…

(Martha enters. Teya puts his hands together and silently pleads with her. She exits.)

LUKE: The story "Changing the Dog" is in your book, *Stories from a Lost Heritage*. I had forgotten it, but my Milosh reminded me about it just before he left. He wanted to order a taxi to the airport, and so I said: "But, I'm a taxi driver, son." And he said: "You're a taxi driver to other people, to me you're a father." And while he was putting on his shoes, I asked him: "What does that mean, Milosh?" And then he reminded me about the story, "Changing the Dog"…and called a taxi.

The Psychic Life of Savages
Amy Freed

Scene: Here and now
    3 Men: Ted Magus (30s) a young English poet, Dr. Robert Stoner (60s) American Poet Laureate and a radio interviewer.

Here, two self-absorbed and convoluted poets jam on a college radio show.

O   O   O

(A radio station. Ted Magus, Dr. Robert Stoner, and Interviewer are on the air.)

INTERVIEWER: Welcome to Potshots. I'm interviewing Britain's Ted Magus and our own American Poet Laureate Dr. Robert Stoner here at Wardwell College. Mr. Magus, you say, in your introduction to *Songs of the Fen*, "Bark and bleat. Reach into your own darkness and remember how to howl. Ask the beasts. Ask the birds." What does that mean?

TED: Call to a hawk in a foul black wind, and have him scream his answer to you. I have.

INTERVIEWER: What are you suggesting—?

TED: I'm sure Dr. Stoner would share my belief that the poet is the shaman, chosen to heal our soul-sick society—

STONER: I couldn't agree less.

TED: Oh, really?

INTERVIEWER: Would you like to say more about that, Dr. Stoner?

STONER: No.

INTERVIEWER: Mr. Magus. You consistently use nature as metaphor—the hawk, a symbol for freedom and release, the cow for domestic stagnation…

TED: A trout don't think when he leap for the sky.

(Pause.)

INTERVIEWER: Let's talk about some of your poetic techniques. Your unique use of rhythm, for example.

TED: Rhythm. It's both awakening and sleep inducing. Trance. The fall-through to the spirit world. I'm very interested in that. Paradox. We are surrounded by paradox. In sleep, we wake. In waking, we sleep. We starve in the midst of plenty. And in fasting, we become full.

STONER: If my aunt had a dick, she'd be my uncle.

TED: Oh, but exactly. Dr. Stoner, you're joking, but the joke is, you've actually touched something far truer—

STONER: Oh, please.

INTERVIEWER: You've said a lot, here, Mr. Magus, let me pick up on what you said about rhythm. Do you actually attempt to induce a trancelike state in the reader?

TED: Well, there's an instance, in the title poem, for example, where I say—

Skirts of the wind sweep
Dry rustle grasses
Shucka—shucka—shucka—
There go me glasses.
Reaching into gassy bog
Bluggah bluggah bluggah—
I hear my heart in
Song of frog
I read my soul
In rotted log
Good night little sleepers, little peepers,
God's sticky creepers—

INTERVIEWER: It seems that there's almost a tribal intensity at the beginning and then it slides imperceptibly towards what's really a hypnotic lullaby near the end.

TED: Exactly.

INTERVIEWER: Extraordinary.

TED: Well, do you know what's even more extraordinary, I came to find out later what I heard in the bog that day was known in ancient Bali as the monkey chant. Identical! It goes—

—shak shaka shak
—shak shaka shaka shaka shak,
—shak shak shak
—shak shaka shaka shaka shak…

INTERVIEWER: Fantastic.

TED: Chanted by hags. Women are more connected with the occult.

INTERVIEWER: Which brings us to you, Dr. Stoner.

STONER: Why?

INTERVIEWER: You said in a recent interview, Dr. Stoner, that you are not convinced of the innocence of the Salem witches.

STONER: There's a lot of room for doubt in my book.

INTERVIEWER: And quite a *book* it's going to be. I doubt any book of poems has been awaited with as much eagerness as your free verse cycle on the life of Cotton Mather. Will you give us a little teaser?

STONER: Well, there is this one little piece I've begun about the witch-girls. Now, I have the image, the spear is in my hand, as it were, but I'm having trouble with the target. Frankly, I think that what with the damned insulin therapy that maybe my focus is a little off, but well, here goes.

Mather knew—
And for this they hated him, all the dark daughters,
Old Cotton, he was blessed with eyes that see 'round corners
Eyes that through God's hard grace could render even
Termites translucent.
With those pale and potent eyes
Mather could see the Witch Girls—

And then it goes something—something—something—. I don't know. And that's where I've been stuck with it for years, now.

(Pause.)

INTERVIEWER: Interesting. The whole process, I mean—

STONER: I can hear the shrill of a high wind, and a chill, like a damp petticoat. Oh, they're around, all right, and they're probably out to fuck me up.

INTERVIEWER: Who, Dr. Stoner?

STONER: The Witch Girls, of course.

INTERVIEWER: What?

TED: *(Slowly, as if feeling his way in a trance.)* One. Mather sees in a dream. A young witch screams astride the bucking buck from Zanzibar. Her ice-cold teat reminds him of his wife.

STONER: Hah hah! Not bad, Son.

TED: Wait! Wait! I'm getting…
—Two. Seen in residue of
Lumpy morning porridge—
Bowl uncleared by slattern daughter,
Does she dance now with the broom—?

STONER: An old witch and a young one
With their mobcaps cast aside
Stand in skanky petticoats
Bare toes sunk in stable muck—
Hold a jar,
It's full of winter wheat—
And something fat and white.
Floating closer, Father Mather sees

His member, long and hungry—!
Too large to be a maggot, with that freckle on the tip!
TED: *(Angry and excited.)* Mather, in a lather, now
Knows the way is stony
But that fire will be the answer,
If he wants his penis back!
STONER: My boy! My boy! My boy!
INTERVIEWER: We've just witnessed an astonishing improvisation between two remarkable poets, it seems to have surprised them as much as it did me, they're embracing now, on the stage floor, much moved, much emotion, and Ted Magus is now drumming in what seems to be a tribute to the senior poet, who has his eyes closed and is covered in sweat. Our time is up and—astonishing program—goodnight, this was Potshots, live from Wardwell College.
TED AND STONER: Shak shak shak shak shaka shaka shaka shak!
Shak shak shak shak shaka shaka shaka shak!

The Queen's Knight

Frank Cossa

Scene: Paris, October 1793

    2 Men: Fouquier-Tinville (50s) the Public Prosecutor of the Revolutionary Tribunal and Chauveau-Lagarde (27) the attorney selected to defend Marie-Antoinette.

The idealistic young Chauveau-Lagarde has been summoned to Paris for the purpose of defending the former Queen before the Tribunal. Here, he confronts Fouquier-Tinville, a former mentor, with the fact that such a trial would be nothing but a sham.

O   O   O

(Paris. The home of the Public Prosecutor Fouquier-Tinville. He sits at his desk writing by candlelight.
A loud knocking. Fouquier-Tinville looks up and smiles to himself, then continues writing. The sound of locks, then of voices. Enter Chauveau-Lagarde. Fouquier-Tinville ignores him.)

CHAUVEAU-LAGARDE: You sent for me, monsieur?

FOUQUIER: You know why?

CHAUVEAU-LAGARDE: No.

FOUQUIER: You're the last to know then.

CHAUVEAU-LAGARDE: Why was I summoned here tonight?

FOUQUIER: *(Looking up.)* You're very impatient.

CHAUVEAU-LAGARDE: I merely ask…

FOUQUIER: Poor Chauveau-Lagarde. He is annoyed at having to leave his comfortable house in the country, and travel to Paris on a rainy night. *(Pause.)* Did you bring your lovely wife?

CHAUVEAU-LAGARDE: No.

FOUQUIER: Pity. She does make things seem…brighter.

CHAUVEAU-LAGARDE: You should know.

FOUQUIER: I *do* know. You *should* know, but you don't.

CHAUVEAU-LAGARDE: Was I sent for to discuss my domestic arrangements?

FOUQUIER: No. The Revolutionary Tribunal has need of you. You are to be given a task worthy of your high opinion of yourself. You know that the former Queen is to be tried?

CHAUVEAU-LAGARDE: I have heard rumors…

FOUQUIER: They are true…

CHAUVEAU-LAGARDE: But what has that to do with—

FOUQUIER:…and you have been appointed to defend her.

(Silence. Fouquier writes scratchily with his quill, Chauveau-Lagarde hesitates.)

CHAUVEAU-LAGARDE: I am afraid that I—

FOUQUIER: Nonsense. Whatever else you are, you are never afraid. That is well known.

CHAUVEAU-LAGARDE: I must decline.

FOUQUIER: *(Almost smiling.)* Decline? You are not being consulted, you have been appointed. It is done.

CHAUVEAU-LAGARDE: Why have a trial at all? The outcome is certain.

FOUQUIER: The outcome will be legal and just.

CHAUVEAU-LAGARDE: And then you will cut off her head.

FOUQUIER: *(Looking up.)* That is not a wholesome attitude. Be careful, monsieur.

CHAUVEAU-LAGARDE: Why me?

FOUQUIER: You are the perfect choice. You have remained aloof from our glorious struggle. You pledge loyalty to the new order but you keep your aristocratic name and your fine country house. It is time you came down from your Olympian height, monsieur, it is time you took part.

CHAUVEAU-LAGARDE: In what? A sham trial? A legal murder?

FOUQUIER: *(Angry.)* You will serve the will of the people!

CHAUVEAU-LAGARDE: A rioting mob?

FOUQUIER: *(Shouting.)* The will of the people is supreme here! It will not be challenged by some milky intellectual. *(Jumping to his feet, screaming, shaking out of control.)* We do not quibble over fine points of law here, we unleash thunder! We do not condemn kings, we plunge them into the void! And with them all the effeminate aristocrats, all the lecherous priests, all the simpering intellectuals who stand in our way! *(He calms himself and sits down.)* Now you have angered me. I do not like to be angry. *(He writes, then folds the paper and hands it to Chauveau-Lagarde.)* This is a letter which will admit you to the Conciergerie where you may see the prisoner. I would do it soon if I were you. The trial begins at eight o'clock tomorrow morning.

CHAUVEAU-LAGARDE: *(Stunned.)* You can't mean that.

FOUQUIER: *(Back to work, detached as before.)* I mean everything I say, as you know.

CHAUVEAU-LAGARDE: But I haven't even seen the charge.

FOUQUIER: Oh, yes. You see how distracted you make me. *(Opens a drawer, takes out a sheaf of papers and hands them to him.)*

CHAUVEAU-LAGARDE: When am I to study all this?

FOUQUIER: Tonight.

CHAUVEAU-LAGARDE: And question the prisoner?

FOUQUIER: Tonight.

CHAUVEAU-LAGARDE: And find witnesses for the defense?

FOUQUIER: Tonight. Though I don't think you'll find many of those. The former Queen's loyal supporters all seem to have fled the country.

CHAUVEAU-LAGARDE: How can I prepare a defense in one night?

FOUQUIER: You're the brilliant young advocate, not me. I am only a simple public servant trying to do my duty. You would be wise to do the same.

CHAUVEAU-LAGARDE: I see. I'm to act in a charade, a kind of dumb show for the sake of…of what? Posterity? History? Who are you trying to impress? As you say, there is no one to speak for the Queen. Why don't you just send somebody over to slit her throat in the night and be done with it? Or would that deprive the mob of their daily entertainment, their spectacle…

FOUQUIER: You're becoming melodramatic again, monsieur. I would remind you that your time is short.

CHAUVEAU-LAGARDE: Just long enough to compromise everything I believe.

FOUQUIER: Stop your platitudes and listen to me. You are already on file with the chief of police as a holder of dangerous views…

CHAUVEAU-LAGARDE: To whom are my views dangerous?

FOUQUIER: To you! However the Committee of Public Safety is prepared to guarantee your well-being if…

CHAUVEAU-LAGARDE: The Committee of Public Safety can't even guarantee its own safety, let alone mine. The mob rules here, and where the mob rules no one can be safe for long. Not even you.

FOUQUIER: *(Starts to rise again, sits down, and laughs.)* Oh, you do amuse me. If I thought you believed half of what you say I would have prosecuted you long ago. But as I know you believe *all* of what you say. I can only conclude that you are quite mad and therefore not worth worrying about. Good evening, monsieur.

(As Chauveau Lagarde exits.)

FOUQUIER: Regards to your wife.

Sonny Deree's Life
Passes Before His Eyes
Bill Bozzone

Scene: Present, motel room off New Jersey turnpike
    2 Men: Sonny Deree (45), bookmaker and Mick Reilly (24), hired killer.

Sonny is about to be executed by Mick for failure to pay a debt. He desperately seeks a way out.

SONNY: *(Into the phone.)*…yeah! Right! Sonny DeRee! From P.S. 181! We sat next to one another in Earth Science! *(He listens.)* Right! Cangelosi's class! *(Beat.)* Good, and you?! *(Short pause.)* Andrew, listen, I don't have a lot of time to reminisce, so let me get right to the point. I need nine-thousand dollars and I need it like immediately…*(Pause.)* Andrew? *(Sonny sighs, hangs up, puts the phone down.)* This is ridiculous. You might as well kill me right now.

MICK: Okay. *(Mick stands, grabs the pull-cord on the chain saw.)*

SONNY: No! Wait! I didn't mean that! What I mean is, give me a little more time! Another couple of hours! Something could still come through!

MICK: Like what?

SONNY: I don't know! Something!

MICK: Time is a problem for me, Sonny. It really is. *Metallica* is playing the Forum tonight and I haven't even picked up my ticket.

SONNY: What has that got to do with anything?!

MICK: I kill you right now, I'm out of here in five minutes, I avoid the headaches of rush hour.

(Sonny indicates the chain saw.)

SONNY: Why do you have to use that thing? Why can't you conduct business with a gun like everybody else?!

MICK: The chain saw is my trademark, Sonny. It's something I'm associated with. People see the hit, they see the condition of the deceased, they say, "This looks like Mick Reilly was here."

SONNY: *(Approaches.)* Mick. Listen. You and I have been pretty close friends over the years.

MICK: We have?

SONNY: Come on, man. We've broken bread to[...] been like brothers.

(Mick shrugs.)

SONNY: Donnie-Boy's wedding reception. Did we or a[...] together the entire time?

MICK: I didn't even know you were there.

SONNY: Of course I was there! You remember! I kept trying to bu[...] cigarette off you! Except that you knew I was trying to quit and you wouldn't give me one!

MICK: I was looking out for your health.

SONNY: Yes!

MICK: Ironic, huh?

SONNY: Please, Mick. Lend me the nine grand.

MICK: I can't do that, Sonny. What kind of hit man would I be if I did that? It would set a negative example. It would encourage other people in the future. I would be less like a hired killer and more like Phil Rizutto of the Money Store.

SONNY: Okay, forget the money! How about this! You could *say* you killed me and who would know? I'd leave the state! I swear to God! Nobody would ever hear a peep from me again!

MICK: I can't do that.

SONNY: Why not?!

MICK: Because this is my job, Sonny. I do it to the best of my ability. (Pause.) You know where I was 13 months ago? Blimpies. And friends would come in—my own sister would come in—and expect something for nothing. But I never played that, Sonny. People with me always get what they pay for. No more, no less.

SONNY: (Nervous laugh.) I'd like to think I'm a little more important than extra dressing on a wedge.

MICK: You'd like to, but in this case, you're not. (Pause.) So. Anything. you want before I start? Glass of water, couple of Tylenol?

SONNY: One more phone call. (Sonny quickly moves to the phone book.)

MICK: Come on, Sonny. You've already called everybody.

SONNY: Not everybody. (Sonny pages frantically through the book.) I saw a name in here last night. "DeRay." Could be a slight variation of my own. Some distant relative.

MICK: (Approaches.) Sonny, have a heart. Fifteen more minutes and I hit the Newark Airport crowd.

SONNY: Just take a minute.

mean to harp on this, but I have a certain phobia when it comes
_ic_. Relates to my father who was himself killed on the Long Island
Expressway.

(Sonny finds the name in the book.)

MICK: Ironically, he was on foot at the time.

(Sonny starts to dial.)

MICK: His car had broken down and he was looking for help, and I guess he wasn't paying attention to where he was walking. Wandered right out in front of a bus and was squashed like a tomato.

(Sonny waits.)

MICK: Teaches you a valuable lesson, though. *(Pause.)* If you ever break down on the Long Island Expressway? Stay with your vehicle.

SONNY: *(Into phone.)* Hello?! Who is this?! *(Listens.)* "Janine." *(Beat.)* Is your mommy or daddy home, Janine? *(Beat.)* He is. *(Beat.)* He's sleeping. *(Beat.)* Could you wake him up for me, please? *(Beat.)* Why not? *(Beat.)* Janine, honey, this is very important. I promise he won't get mad. *(Beat.)* Because I just know. *(Beat.)* Because he would want you to wake him up. *(Beat.)* *Because I'm dying, Janine!*

(Mick goes to Sonny, takes the phone receiver from him.)

MICK: That's it.

SONNY: *(Into phone as Mick takes it away.)* You hear that man, Janine?! He has a chain saw! *Don't make me send him over to your house tonight while you're sleeping, Janine…!*

(Mick hangs up the phone.)

MICK: Let's just do it.

(Mick takes the saw, yanks the pull-cord. The saw comes to life. Mick takes a step or two toward Sonny who falls on his knees, closes his eyes, brings his hands together.)

What Rough Beast Slouches
Brad Fairchild

Scene: Berlin, early in the 20th century

2 Men: Maximilian Harden (30-40) idealistic editor of *The Future,* a Berlin weekly paper, and Philipp Eulenburg (30-40) diplomat, composer and closest friend of Kaiser William II, last emperor of Germany.

When the close relationship between the Kaiser and Philipp Eulenburg begins to cause a scandal in Berlin society, the self-righteous Harden meets with Philipp and attempts to blackmail him into leaving Germany.

(Late at night in a park. Two benches close together. Harden is pacing, waiting for someone. He takes out his pocket watch but cannot see the time in the dark, so he holds it to the moonlight to make out the hour.)

HARDEN: Damn it. Where is he. *(Philipp enters.)*

PHILIPP: Mr. Harden.

HARDEN: My letter said ten.

PHILIPP: I couldn't get away. You're lucky I came at all.

HARDEN: Oh, what luck! Yours is the face I most long to see at night before I sleep.

PHILIPP: What do you want? It's late.

HARDEN: I thought a night meeting would suit your nocturnal proclivities.

PHILIPP: *(Starts to leave.)* Good night, Mr. Harden.

HARDEN: Eulenberg, wait. I want to make a deal with you.

PHILIPP: A deal? What makes you think you have anything I want?

HARDEN: I know I do.

Now, most people in your situation would just have a gang of thugs beat the shit out of the nasty little editor, but I know you don't have the stomach for that kind of thing. So I'm offering you another way out.

PHILIPP: I assume this has to do with your recent articles.

HARDEN: How astute of you.

PHILIPP: I'm afraid you've got it all wrong.

HARDEN: I don't think so.

PHILIPP: I know you do!

HARDEN: You think my information is incorrect?

PHILIPP: You just misunderstand—

HARDEN: Misunderstand?

PHILIPP: Yes.

HARDEN: What the hell's to misunderstand? Who does what to whom? Let's see, where am I unclear? You couldn't be the one on top?

PHILIPP: What are you talking about?

HARDEN: Perversity.

PHILIPP: You actually think that.

HARDEN: Of the worst kind.

PHILIPP: Do you enjoy ruining people's lives?

HARDEN: It's called the truth.

PHILIPP: Oh, the truth! Doesn't that involve at least considering both sides?

HARDEN: Not really.

PHILIPP: You're a journalist. You have an obligation to listen—

HARDEN: My obligation is to the future. Nothing else! The physical and moral health of this nation. And if that means I don't take your precious feelings into consideration, then so be it! Fuck your nasty side of things!

PHILIPP: No matter who it hurts?

HARDEN: No matter who!

PHILIPP: Even if they're not guilty?

HARDEN: You're not innocent, don't even try.

PHILIPP: I'm not ashamed of anything.

HARDEN: A little shame would do you good.

PHILIPP: And you?

HARDEN: What?

PHILIPP: A little shame?

HARDEN: Shame is what fuels this whole fucking mess. I am ashamed. Of you, him, the rest of your sickening friends—how can Germany hold her head up?

PHILIPP: The Kaiser makes you sick?

HARDEN: If he does, it's your fault.

PHILIPP: And ashamed?

HARDEN: I know where you're going with this. The Kaiser is not Germany.

PHILIPP: You're avoiding the question. Are you loyal to the Kaiser?

HARDEN: If the pilot steers too close to the rocks, the course must be corrected.

PHILIPP: What does that have to do with me?!

HARDEN: Night after night, thrashing around in lustful ecstasy on William's sweaty sheets! Singing that wicked siren's song into his naked ear. Lorelei—that creature—writhing in wet glee on the side of the river mountain—calling all of us to our deaths.

PHILIPP: That's ridiculous.

HARDEN: Don't pretend.

PHILIPP: You've got no proof.

HARDEN: You'd be surprised how cheaply spying servants come these days.

PHILIPP: Who is the public going to believe?

HARDEN: Seeds are planted.

PHILIPP: I've never done anything to compromise this country's well-being.

HARDEN: No?

PHILIPP: Never. I love Germany at least as much as you claim to.

HARDEN: You love nothing but yourself. That's the character of your kind. I don't know if it's even something you can control. But your perversity can't be permitted to reign unchecked, to spread, like a virus, to innocent people, infecting the moral health of society. That's the death of a state. You must at least realize that?

The death of a state.

PHILIPP: Mr. Harden, you don't know what I feel. I know love.

HARDEN: You mistake things. Misguided sexual desire is not love.

PHILIPP: I love him. I love Germany. As God is in Heaven.

HARDEN: There is no God in your Heaven.

PHILIPP: Good night, Mr. Harden.

HARDEN: Go then. But I feel it's only fair to warn you that my articles will continue as long as necessary. I can't have you destroying our armed forces and leaving us vulnerable to the rest of Europe. As long as you keep at it, I will keep writing.

PHILIPP: You don't scare me.

HARDEN: I scare the Kaiser.

PHILIPP: I assure you, he doesn't read your trash.

HARDEN: He'll hear about it soon enough.

PHILIPP: Haven't you accomplished your goal?

HARDEN: Which is what?

PHILIPP: To hurt me.

HARDEN: To hurt you?

PHILIPP: To hurt me!

HARDEN: You still don't understand. I don't want to hurt anyone.

This morning, on my way to the paper, I saw a young woman out in front of her window. She was beating a rat to death with a broom. Just over and over and over. Swinging at the vermin. The broom was turning red, with blood. It was...I didn't even want to watch. The complete violence of the whole thing. She had to do it. Kill the rat. I understood. She had to kill it or it would keep coming back inside her house, threatening her children, stealing her food. She had to kill it because—

PHILIPP: What do you want from me?

HARDEN: I want you to quit meddling in state affairs—

PHILIPP: Really, you seem to have the wrong idea—

HARDEN: Selling Germany out to protect your dear little position of privilege.

PHILIPP: I think you exaggerate my influence.

HARDEN: Don't act so guileless. You don't fool me. You fill the Kaiser's head with visions of personal grandeur so that he feels the need to rule like some sort of medieval king with no regard for democratic principle of any kind.

PHILIPP: If you're what democratic principle leads to—

HARDEN: Yes, I am.

PHILIPP: —then I want none of it.

HARDEN: And the people want none of you. You have a single option. Leave the Kaiser. Leave Berlin.

PHILIPP: What?

HARDEN: Leave.

PHILIPP: Leave? How dare you—

HARDEN: Immediately.

PHILIPP: You are out of your mind to think you can blackmail me.

HARDEN: You will go.

PHILIPP: I will not.

HARDEN: You will never see or speak to the Kaiser again, or more and more of the perverse details of your private life will find their way to the public. How will you feel then? When every sordid sin is spelled out in the headlines? When the people turn against him? When he's forced to give up his throne? How will you feel knowing you were the cause?

PHILIPP: I refuse to listen to any more of this—

HARDEN: Knowing. Having it eat away at you year after year that you ruined his life because of your selfishness. Do you think he'd ever be able to think about you in the same way again? His touch would grow cold. Every time he looked at you all he would feel is regret. Don't take his kingdom. Because if you do, you take what's most important to him. You will go.

PHILIPP: To hell with you!

HARDEN: If you stay we all lose.

PHILIPP: I lose either way. So why not choose to do what leaves me with my integrity intact.

HARDEN: Would you care so much about your own fate if you really loved him?

PHILIPP: My love for William and for Germany is the source of my resolve.

HARDEN: Believe me, before I'm through, that resolve will crumble into a hundred insignificant pieces.

Alphabet of Flowers

Elyse Nass

Scene: A park bench
   2 Women: Jean (60) and Kate (60), childhood friends/lovers having a reunion after forty
   years.

Kate's parents sent her away to a midwestern college in an effort to end her relationship with Jean. Forty years later, the two women meet as they vowed to—on the last day of September of their 60th year. Here, Kate reveals with great difficulty that she never stopped loving Jean.

○   ○   ○

JEAN: I'd say, let's do this again…meet in another forty years…If we're around, we'll be 100…And who knows what we'll be like then?

KATE: I'm sure we'll have more wrinkles. Maybe I'll have cataracts…And most definitely, osteoporosis.

JEAN: And we'll probably be walking with canes…Although I would use a silver walking stick.

KATE: I bet you would look elegant.

JEAN: Thank you.

KATE: And the tree…I bet it won't be here.

JEAN: I'm sure it won't be. *(Pause.)* Now that would be a far-fetched meeting to plan…

KATE: It would be crazy.

(Pause.)

JEAN: You know, it was good to see you—

KATE: The same here.

JEAN: Both of us, sharing our lives, after such a long time.

KATE: I want to thank you for sharing your life with me.

JEAN: And yours with me…We met, told our stories, now it's time to leave. *(Pause.)* Will you tell your parents about our meeting today?

KATE: I think I will.

JEAN: They'll be surprised. I'm sure. I know they would remember me. They'll probably want to know why you bothered to come here and you might say, for old time's sake.

(Pause.)

KATE: It seems to have gotten chilly, suddenly.

JEAN: You're right. *(Pause.)* Anyway, it's been a real pleasure, Kate. Give my very best to your parents.

KATE: I will.

(Jean turns to go.)

KATE: Jean?

JEAN: Yes?

KATE: You're going?

JEAN: Yes.

KATE: Perhaps I'll never see you again.

JEAN: Don't tell me you want to meet again in forty years? Even I wouldn't be that absurd.

KATE: No, it's not that. It's—

JEAN: Our meeting is over, Kate.

KATE: I know it is. But I wanted to tell you something…something else…something I didn't tell you during our meeting…something I came here to tell you… Up till the very end of the meeting, I couldn't tell you. You see, it's very difficult for me… I hope you understand I came here today because more than half my life is over.

JEAN: Is there something wrong with you, Kate? Are you ill?

KATE: No, I'm fine. I meant in terms of years left to live.

JEAN: When you look at it that way, so is mine.

KATE: When I saw you walking away, I thought, if I don't say it now, maybe I'll never have the chance. I should have said it before…You see…I did think about you…during my early years of marriage.

JEAN: Yes, you told me.

KATE: Sometimes I would get myself flowers, all kinds of flowers…and remember that's what you would sometimes do…for me…*(Pause.)* You asked me why I came here today. I said, there were a few reasons. One was curiosity. I also came back to apologize, leaving the way I did, never being in touch. You have every right to be angry.

JEAN: I'm not angry. I told you I have no bad feelings.

KATE: You asked me why I came here today.

JEAN: And you've told me.

KATE: I must have a cigarette now. I haven't smoked all this time… Now I need a cigarette.

JEAN: Just one.

KATE: *(Lighting up.)* Just one. *(Pause.)* Marriage was right for me at that time. But I guess my feelings were still there.

JEAN: What feelings?

KATE: The feelings I kept inside of me… I tried not to think about them. Sometimes I thought my veins were about to burst…that the blood in my body was about to pour out… All through my marriage…there were voices screaming inside my head but I managed to shut them up… But after years of marriage, thirty-one years, I was losing the battle. I couldn't be there for Ken anymore…emotionally, sexually… I got a divorce.

JEAN: What are you saying?

KATE: I still had those feelings for you. I thought about you… When I was with him, sometimes I'd fantasize being with you again…then it went away…but it would always come back.

JEAN: All those years, you kept all that inside. How could you?

KATE: I did.

JEAN: If you had those feelings, why didn't you get a divorce sooner?

KATE: In the 50s, women were married and had children. That was the way it was. I had my college degree but I never pursued any career. I was married at twenty, remember. After the 50s, then came the 60s, the 70s, and I was still feeling stuck but was still too terrified. Then it was the 80s…I started smoking three packs a day…the chain-smoking wife…tearing at my hair.

JEAN: Oh, Kate.

KATE: Now do you think of my life as one of privilege?

JEAN: No, it was one of punishment. *(Pause.)* Did you tell your husband why you wanted a divorce?

KATE: I couldn't. I just said simply, "Our marriage seems to have come to an end after thirty-one years."

JEAN: You couldn't even tell him.

KATE: No. *(Pause.)* After my divorce, I thought about meeting someone… going to a woman's bar…or a meeting. Then I thought, at my age? I was fifty-one. *(Pause.)* I would read about all the groups…and all the meetings… all the events…some for older women… Yet I still couldn't bring myself to go. Then I thought about our meeting, the one that was arranged ages ago…I couldn't wait for it…I was hoping you'd show up. And you did. I had to find out…if those feelings I had would still be there…So I came back here today… I thought, if I see you, would those feelings come back from years ago?

JEAN: And did they?

KATE: They did.

(Pause.)

JEAN: Let me sit down.

KATE: Do you want a cigarette?

JEAN: No, I don't smoke.

KATE: Of course you don't. *(Pause.)* Sometimes…you'd give me flowers. All kinds of flowers, and they smelled like exotic perfume. We read e.e. cummings and listened to jazz. You wrote me letters. We made love. It was the first time for both of us. They say you always remember the first time. That is the only truly special time in your life.

JEAN: Yes. *(Pause.)* I don't know what to say. Out of a movie?

KATE: Yes, I was going to say that.

JEAN: Now I'm beginning to think it really is. Two ex-lovers meet when they're sixty and…?

Dolly Would

Jocelyn Beard

Scene: Inside a car heading from Waxahatchie, TX, to Dollywood

    2 Women: Dolly D. and Dolly Z. (20s), two friends heading out on a vacation that becomes an adventure.

An argument over psychic phenomena leads to a greater understanding of love between two friends.

O   O   O

(At rise we find two women, Dolly D. and Dolly Z. Both are dressed as Dolly Parton, complete with wigs and showy country western duds. They are traveling in a car. Dolly Z. drives while Dolly D. leafs through a stack of travel brochures.)

DOLLY D.: Hey, listen to this! *(Reads from brochure.)* "Visit Uncle Reverend Jimmy Joe Bob's Bible World, just off I-70, and be reborn into the Divine Light of the Lord for $39.99 plus tax. Don't forget to pay a quick visit to our drive-thru Church of Absolution."

DOLLY Z.: Where'd you get that?

DOLLY D.: Momma picked it up for me down at Bob's on the strip.

DOLLY Z.: Bob the travel agent?

DOLLY D.: Yup.

DOLLY Z.: Sheeee-it.

DOLLY D.: *(Holding up the huge stack of travel brochures.)* She got a copy of every brochure for every attraction between Waxahatchie and Dollywood.

DOLLY Z.: Sheeee-it.

DOLLY D.: I told her, I said: "Momma, Dolly Z. and I ain't gonna be havin' no time to be stoppin' at no attractions." And do you know what she said to me?

DOLLY Z.: Nope.

DOLLY D.: I'm gonna tell you. She said, "Dolly D., darlin', you don't have no time to begin with, so do yourself a favor and see what ya can while ya can." What d'you spose she meant by that?

DOLLY Z.: By what?

DOLLY D.: That we ain't got no time to begin with. What d'you spose she meant by that?

DOLLY Z.: I spose she meant that we got no time.

DOLLY D.: Naw, not "Queen Cryptic." Everything that woman says has a kind of a hidden meaning.

DOLLY Z.: Then why don't you just ask her what she means when she says it.

DOLLY D.: Whaddya mean, when she says it?

DOLLY Z.: I mean when the words are actually coming out of her mouth! Sheee-it, Dolly D.!

DOLLY D.: Anyway, I thought this place sounded kinda interesting.

DOLLY Z.: What place?

DOLLY D.: *(Holding up brochure.)* Mini-Graceland.

DOLLY Z.: Mini-Graceland?

DOLLY D.: Uh-huh. *(Reads.)* Mini-Graceland. The world's only fully miniature Graceland, complete with gardens and family plot...oh, lookit that, Dolly Z., a teeny tiny Elvis gravestone!

DOLLY Z.: His name's spelt wrong.

DOLLY D.: *(Peering at photo on brochure.)* How the hell can you see that from there?

DOLLY Z.: No, at the real Graceland. They spelt his name wrong on the gravestone.

DOLLY D.: Get out! They fix it?

DOLLY Z.: Nope.

DOLLY D.: Damn!

DOLLY Z.: Amen.

DOLLY D.: No wonder people see him all over creation.

DOLLY Z.: Meanin'?

DOLLY D.: Meanin' he's pissed off about his name being spelt wrong on the gravestone!

DOLLY Z.: Sheee-it, Dolly D.

DOLLY D.: What do you mean: "Sheee-it, Dolly D.?"

DOLLY Z.: You know exactly what I meant. There ain't no one on God's green earth who's seen hide nor hair of Elvis Presley since the day they found him with his head in the toilet.

DOLLY D.: *(Warning.)* Don't go there, Dolly Z.

DOLLY Z.: Don't get yourself in a state.

DOLLY D.: I mean it! I ain't goin there with you. I just ain't prepared for another one of your lectures.

DOLLY Z.: Lectures!

DOLLY D.: That's right, that's what I said! Every time I try to bring up anything havin' anything to do with my spiritual and highly psychic nature, you just can't resist lecturin' me about how dumb you think I am!

DOLLY Z.: Ain't true!

DOLLY D.: Is too!

DOLLY Z.: Not!

DOLLY D.: Okay, do you or do you not doubt the fact that Margie-Joe Cantwell saw a vision of River Phoenix floatin' above the fountain at the Tri-City Mall last month?

DOLLY Z.: Dolly D., you know damn well that Margie-Joe Cantwell ain't been the same since the accident.

DOLLY D.: Hittin' her head on that loading ramp opened her up to the world of psychic phenomena!

DOLLY Z.: She's got a metal plate in her head.

DOLLY D.: She hears voices from beyond!

DOLLY Z.: *(Scornfully.)* That plate tunes in Superstation 7 on Sunday mornings.

DOLLY D.: Right! On *Sunday* morning!

DOLLY Z.: Sheee-it, Dolly D. I spose you'd believe me if I told you that *I* saw a vision of River Phoenix!

DOLLY D.: Oh my Sweet Jesus! How did he look?

DOLLY Z.: Get a grip, girlfriend. You see, this is exactly what I was trying to tell you last Wednesday at canasta when you said that you had an ESP vision of my hand and we *lost*.

DOLLY D.: I ain't gonna listen to no damn lecture on my vacation! I've been waitin' for this for a whole year. It's the only chance I get to disappear…

DOLLY Z.: It's *our* vacation, Dolly D.! And *I* ain't about to listen to any of your New Age mumbo jumbo!

DOLLY D.: Dolly Z., when are you gonna acknowledge your spiritual self?

DOLLY Z.: When and if I get one!

DOLLY D.: Oh, you've got one all right. You just don't open yourself up to it!

DOLLY Z.: If you mean by "open myself up" that I should pay my hard-earned money to that old fake…

DOLLY D.: Madam Xera ain't no fake!

DOLLY Z.:…money that I work damn hard for…

DOLLY D.: You run the cash register at Sterlings Variety Store.

DOLLY Z.: So? At least it's honest work! At least I don't rake it in by tellin' people that because a *card*—a piece of paper with a drawin' on it—landed a certain way on my table that they're gonna receive an inheritance, or have a baby, or find love at the laundromat!

DOLLY D.: That is so unfair, Dolly Z! Madam Xera said "dry cleaners!" I have it on tape!

DOLLY Z.: Then why did you spend that en-tire day at the Lonesome Pine Laundromat?

DOLLY D.: I screwed up, okay? I just got so excited when Madam Xera told me that my romantic destiny would be waitin' for me where I got my clothes cleaned that I wasn't thinkin' straight! And anyways, how does me spendin' the day at the laundromat prove that you don't have a spiritual self? Hmmm?

DOLLY Z.: I'll tell you what it does prove! It proves that you weren't bein' entirely honest with poor Eddie Nichols when you accepted his pre-engagement ring!

DOLLY D.: Dolly Z., you know good and well that Eddie Nichols in no way represents my romantic destiny!

DOLLY Z.: I wish you could hear how ridiculous you sound, Dolly Evangeline DuBois!

DOLLY D.: That's right, change the subject. The fact is that you do have a spiritual self and I can prove it!

DOLLY Z.: Oh, please.

DOLLY D.: No, I mean it, Dolly Z.! For starters, why are we goin' on this trip?

DOLLY Z.: We take a vacation this time every year!

DOLLY D.: That's right, but where are we goin' this year?

DOLLY Z.: *(With great exasperation.)* You know dang well where we're goin'.

DOLLY D.: Just say it!

DOLLY Z.: All right! All right! I'll say it! Dollywood! We're goin' to Dollywood!

DOLLY D.: And why are we goin' to Dollywood?

DOLLY Z.: Because that's where we decided to go on vacation this year!

DOLLY D.: Now you think back, Dolly Z. Think back to that afternoon at the food court when we decided.

DOLLY Z.: What's to think about? You said let's go to Dollywood and I said okay!

DOLLY D.: Shame on you, Dorothea Zutz! It didn't happen that way at all!

DOLLY Z.: I didn't say okay? I said something else? Like what? Did I say, let's go to the Riviera?

DOLLY D.: No…

DOLLY Z.: The Congo?

DOLLY D.: No…

DOLLY Z.: What's that place with the UFOs…Machuu Pichuu?

DOLLY D.: No, no *no!*

DOLLY Z.: What then!?

DOLLY D.: You said, where do you want to go this year and I said, someplace special. So you said, how about Nashville and I said nahh, let's go someplace we've never been before. So you said okay, let's go someplace that's special for both of us and I said, great, where would that be? Dollywood, you shoot right back. Dollywood's the place. And of course it is the place what with us both bein' Dolly's an' all. Well, you're not a true Dolly, but you've been known as a Dolly for so long it hardly matters. I mean, who won the 1988 Waxahatchie Dolly Lookalike? You did! I mean, sure, I won '89 through '93 but that's jus' on account of my…well, you know. *(Looks down at her chest.)* After all, how did the two of us meet in the first place? At Elwin Castor's Halloween party, remember? I was "9-5" Dolly and you were "Best Whorehouse" Dolly. Then the next year we both went as "Rhinestone" Dolly's!

DOLLY Z.: I hope there's a point that you're gettin' to.

DOLLY D.: *(Annoyed.)* The point *is,* that your spiritual self tuned right in on the fact that you and me—the two biggest Dolly fans in the en-tire world—and Dolly's ourselves to boot, should go to Dollywood! You're as spiritually connected to Dolly as I am, you jus' won't admit it!

DOLLY Z.: For cryin' out loud, Dolly D.! In the first place, it was you wanted to go to Dollywood, and in the second place, we ain't goin' there because we're "spiritually connected" to Dolly, we're goin' on account of the fact that it ain't that far and we ain't never been there. All I admit is that you've gone loco…

DOLLY D.: Don't say it! Don't say anything that you're liable to regret, Dolly Z. We got a long ride ahead of us.

DOLLY Z.: *(With a sigh.)* You're right. Read me some more of them brochures.

DOLLY D.: *(Brightening.)* Sure! *(Looking through brochures.)* Okay, how about this one: "Jumpin' Gator Jamboree. Over One Thousand Alligators. Shows on the Hour."

DOLLY Z.: Ain't that gator place in Florida?

DOLLY D.: *(Squinting at brochure.)* Hey, you're right…*(Flipping through brochures.)*…well, I'll be…shee-it, Dolly Z! None of these places are anywhere near where we're goin' to!

DOLLY Z.: *(Chuckling.)* You're kidding.

DOLLY D.: Not. *(Reading.)* Oregon, Massachusetts, why, that Mini-Graceland is in Utah—Utah for chrissakes!—Michigan, Delaware…now what in the big blue balls of God did my mother mean by givin' us these brochures?

DOLLY Z.: I think she meant exactly what she said.

DOLLY D.: Now don't *you* start goin' cryptic on me, Dolly Z.

DOLLY Z.: "See whatcha can while ya can."

DOLLY D.: *(Nearly wailing.)* But what does that *mean???*

DOLLY Z.: It means, Dolly D., that you can't shit without a plan, and if you can't come up with one by yourself then you trot on down to Madam Xera and she gives you one. Your ma is jus' tryin' to tell you to stop trying to get from point A and point B so damn fast that you miss everything in between. By givin' you all these different brochures she's tryin' to make you understand that there's more to life than the fate you've planned for yourself.

DOLLY D.: You think I've planned a fate for myself?

DOLLY Z.: A'course. That's why you went to the laundromat when you knew damn well that you were sposed to go the dry cleaners. That's why you pretend not to understand what your momma is sayin' when she's sayin' the plainest thing in the en-tire world. You jus' didn't want to take a chance at changing your fate.

DOLLY D.: And just what, pray tell, is this fate that I've made up for myself?

DOLLY Z.: Well, in about three years you're gonna marry poor Eddie Nichols. In another two you'll quit your job at Burdine's and have a kid or two. Eddie'll get promoted a coupla times at the plant and the two of you will move on up to Burntwood Estates into one of them 3000 square foot houses you think so much of. Kids will grow and you'll do the whole thing with 'em. Cookies, church, scout groups, school trips. Eddie'll start bangin' his secretary but you won't give a shit on account of havin' the house and nice new Caravan. Before you know it, the kids'll take off and you'll finally be able to do the one thing you've wanted to all along.

DOLLY D.: The one thing…?

DOLLY Z.: Disappear, darlin'. You'll finally be able to disappear. You'll just fade into that big 'ole house and all them nice things that Eddie'll provide you with until there's nothing left. Not even Dolly.

(A moment of silence passes as Dolly D. mulls over what Dolly Z. has said.)

DOLLY D.: *(Leafing slowly through brochures.)* You think my momma was tryin' to suggest that there might be a little more of *me* to find out here in these brochures?

DOLLY Z.: Something like that.

DOLLY D.: But, what about you, Dolly Z? Ain't you disappearing too?

DOLLY Z.: Darlin', I dress up like Dolly for exactly two reasons: one. I'm basically pretty fucked-up, and two. it sure beats sittin' around on a Saturday night with my thumb stuck up my be-hind. But know this: Whether I'm Dolly or not don't make no difference to me.

DOLLY D.: So, are you sayin' that you don't want to go to Dollywood?

DOLLY Z.: Hell, I'll go anywhere as long as there's something to see and someone to talk about it with.

(Another moment of silence.)

DOLLY D.: I don't want to disappear.

DOLLY Z.: *(Softly.)* Then don't.

DOLLY D.: Will you help me?

DOLLY Z.: A'course.

DOLLY D.: *(Slyly.)* I appreciate your *spiritual* insight.

DOLLY Z.: *(A warning.)* Dolly…

DOLLY D.: Okay, okay! *(Holding up brochures.)* You'll go anywhere?

DOLLY Z.: Yes, mam.

DOLLY D.: Anywhere?

DOLLY Z.: Are you deaf? I said anywhere and that's exactly what I meant!

DOLLY D.: So, if I throw these brochures up into the air, you'll be happy turnin' this car towards the one that lands on your lap?

DOLLY Z.: How do you know one will land on my lap?

DOLLY D.: Trust me, Dolly Z. One will land on your lap.

DOLLY Z.: Fine.

DOLLY D.: Fine? Does that mean you're puttin' your trust in the Infinite?

DOLLY Z.: Just throw the damn brochures!

DOLLY D.: One last thing. *(She tugs at Dolly Z.'s wig.)* Dolly?

DOLLY Z.: What? You really wanna be us?

DOLLY D.: *(Amazed at the thought.)* I think I do.

(They remove their wigs and suddenly we see two entirely different women who look much younger than they did as Dollys.)

DOLLY D.: You ready?

DOLLY Z.: Toss 'em!

DOLLY D.: Here goes!

(Dolly D. throws the stack of brochures into the air. The two women watch as they flutter back down. They are happy, excited and a little scared.)

Emma's Child

Kristine Thatcher

Scene: Hospital, doctor's office
   2 Women: Jean and Franny.

After a confrontation with Henry, Jean's husband, Jean and Franny have a discussion about motherhood, and what it would mean to be a mother to Emma's child.

○   ○   ○

JEAN: We'll take a bus home.

FRANNY: What do you think you're doing?

JEAN: I'm sorry?

FRANNY: Jean. You can't expect Henry to want to support Robin. The man is forty-six years old. He has one shot at being a father, and he wants it to be a joyful experience.

JEAN: Yes? And?

FRANNY: You don't seriously believe raising Robin would be a joyful experience?

JEAN: Well, you don't, that's clear.

FRANNY: Not every one is cut out to raise a child with special needs. To force Henry to do something against his nature is a betrayal.

JEAN: How can you stand there and talk to *me* about—

FRANNY: What's more, you're betraying yourself!

JEAN: Ah. This is good. How so?

FRANNY: Dammit, Jean, over the years, I've heard in minute detail what you want from motherhood. I'm privy to every secret wish in your head. None of it has anything to do with this boy. This boy will never read. Never chase a cat, or run downstairs on Christmas morning. There will be no idle chat around the kitchen table. He'll never know a woman, never bounce a child on his knee. I am your friend. It seems to me the only thing I can *do* at this point is try to stop you from making a terrible mistake.

JEAN: Once, do you remember—when I was going through all the surgeries and in vitros, when I was exhausted, and we didn't know where else to look for money or support, in an attempt to comfort me, you said, Franny, and I quote: "If you think the journey has been difficult for you, think what it must be like for the child who is trying to get to you." I laughed when you said it;

it sounded so New Age. But, the terrible thing is, you were right! I look at Robin, and see evidence of a harrowing journey.

FRANNY: You don't think I meant this! I only meant to comfort. I never meant for you to chain yourself to the first—

JEAN: Of course you didn't meant this! What kind of idiot would wish for a child with Robin's problems? I wish to god he was healthy! No one ever dreams of this! But, sometimes, this is what comes. In fifteen years of doing everything I can think of to bring a child into my life, this child is the one I've been given. And to my surprise, he's better than anything I *ever* dreamt. I know you think that's crazy, and so does Henry. Because you won't *look*, and if you *don't* look, you won't *get* it. You're afraid of Robin because you think he *is* "his problem." If you come with me, you will see past the deformity, I assure you, to the tremendous person he has had to become in one short month. I am so certain of this, that if you still don't get it, after you've spent one morning with him, I'll walk out of here, away from him for the last time, without one backward glance.

FRANNY: Jean—

JEAN: I'm extending you a privilege. Don't mistake it for anything else.

FRANNY: *(Beat.)* Okay.

(Franny and Jean stand blinking at one another.)

JEAN: What?

FRANNY: I said okay. Lead on. Let's go meet Robin.

(Without further ado, Jean picks up her things and leads Franny out of the room. Blackout.)

German Games
Berrilla Kerr

Scene: A beach house, the present and Germany during W.W.II
  2 Women: Frieda (70s) a woman who fled Germany just before the war and Young Frieda (20s).

Frieda, a Jew, managed to escape the horror of the Holocaust by pretending to be Aryan and running away to Paris with her lover. Here, she muses over those tempestuous days with her younger self.

YOUNG FRIEDA: I feel as if I'm in a great vacuum which I'll never get out of. I want to be grown up. I want to be able to leave. When I'm 18 I'm going to experience everything. I won't be a virgin any longer.

FRIEDA: Gretchen and I put on earrings and pretended we were old enough. We went to a cellar nightclub. It was wild and decadent. We smoked cigarettes and drank beer. There was a jazz trio and a woman dressed in tails who sang.

YOUNG FRIEDA: When an old man leaned against us we decided to leave quick. We pretended we were going to the ladies' room and walked out without paying. We only had two beers, so to hell with them. I found out Jewish boys are different. Gretchen's brother showed us.

FRIEDA: I was being smothered. So I decided on my 18th birthday that I couldn't stand it a moment longer. Something had to happen to me—something different, something new. You and I are the only person who knows.

YOUNG FRIEDA: I hate horses, I hate Wagner, I can't stand Mama. Can't stand her smell anymore—the heavy sickly semi-invalid body odor covered up with crushed rose petals and talcum powder. And Papa and his mistress and his clammy hands.

FRIEDA: I was just fed up with the whole thing.

YOUNG FRIEDA: I saved money, I stole money, I decided to go to Paris.

FRIEDA: Now how could I do it so nobody would know where I was going?

YOUNG FRIEDA: I would go on a hike in the country with Gretchen so I wouldn't be near a phone or anywhere Papa could track me down. He would always call if I left his sight for more than four hours. The problem was clothes—the difference between going to Paris and going on a hike. I managed that by getting out of the house without even Helga seeing me.

FRIEDA: So I found myself on a train on the way to Paris. And there was Otto, sitting across from me, right in my compartment. And next to him a nice old lady with a picnic basket filled with cheese, sausage, fresh-baked bread, fruit and a bottle of wine.

YOUNG FRIEDA: By the time she got off we were deliciously full and warm and happy.

FRIEDA: "What a glorious coincidence," he said, kissing my hand. It got to be dusk…the train speeding past lights. How long was I going to be in Paris? Where would I stay? All these questions I had no answers to.

YOUNG FRIEDA: You're going to lose the button on your jacket.

FRIEDA: He pulled it off and put it in his pocket.

YOUNG FRIEDA: I don't have any francs. I forgot.

FRIEDA: I don't know whether he'd guessed I was running away or not.

YOUNG FRIEDA: Yes you do. He suddenly said, "I'm running away, too. We'll share a cab."

FRIEDA: So there I was in Paris at the Hotel Voltaire. I could open up the doors and look at the Seine.

YOUNG FRIEDA: And Otto was somewhere in the same hotel.

FRIEDA: And I was a virgin, but not for long.

Head On
Elizabeth Dewberry

Scene: Backstage of the Oprah Winfrey Show
    2 Women: Anne (30s) a robust woman and Anne's Therapist (40s) slender and intelligent.

Anne surprises her therapist in the green room of the Oprah Winfrey Show.

O   O   O

(The green room of the Oprah Winfrey show, ten minutes before taping. The therapist paces anxiously, looking at her watch. Anne enters, in shock, and the therapist runs over to her.)

THERAPIST: Oh, thank God you're here. *(Doubletake.)* Anne? What are *you* doing here?

ANNE: I'm sorry I'm late. I saw a wreck.

THERAPIST: But you're not multiorgasmic.

ANNE: No. I'm fine.

THERAPIST: Oh God.

ANNE: I wasn't *in* the wreck. I just saw it happen. I was so afraid I was going to be late. I've wanted to be on *Oprah Winfrey* forever, it's my most recurrent fantasy, and now here I am.

THERAPIST: *Are* you?

ANNE: What?

THERAPIST: Multiorgasmic.

ANNE: I don't think so.

THERAPIST: Who told you to come here?

ANNE: Your receptionist. Do I look bad? I brought another outfit if you don't like this one. This all happened so fast I didn't have time to buy anything. If it hadn't been for the wreck...

THERAPIST: What did she tell you?

ANNE: You were going on Oprah to talk about your book and the client you had coming on with you canceled and would I go on instead.

THERAPIST: Oh God.

ANNE: What? I know I just started seeing you, but you've already been a big help to me, dealing with Jerry's death. I have a lot to say.

THERAPIST: It has to be somebody who's multiorgasmic.

ANNE: Jerry had a bad heart.

THERAPIST: Were you ever multiorgasmic, even by yourself?

ANNE: I never had *one* orgasm. I can't say that on TV. I've never told anybody that before.

THERAPIST: We go on in eight minutes. I can't replace you.

ANNE: It's not my fault. There was a wreck, a head-on collision. But I can do this.

THERAPIST: I know it's not your fault.

ANNE: Two people died. Traffic's still backed up for miles.

THERAPIST: I'm not blaming you. I'm sorry.

ANNE: I'm an official witness, in the police reports. That takes time. Everybody was late to everywhere they were going. Have you ever witnessed a wreck?

THERAPIST: Yes. I have. Can we talk about this later? Right now...

ANNE: Of course. I'm sorry.

THERAPIST: I mean, there's nothing we can do about the wreck.

ANNE: Of course not.

THERAPIST: This was such a great opportunity, *Oprah Winfrey*. I could have been a bestseller. I had this client who was perfect, at age fifty-seven after three months of therapy with me she became multiorgasmic.

ANNE: Why isn't she here?

THERAPIST: She broke her hip.

ANNE: You can break your hip?

THERAPIST: No, she fell in the bathtub.

ANNE: That's too bad.

THERAPIST: It's not the same if you don't have somebody, a real person, to say it works.

ANNE: I'm sorry I haven't read your book, but tell me what to say, and I'll say it. What's the book about?

THERAPIST: Postmenopausal sex.

ANNE: I just wanted to meet Oprah Winfrey. I wanted to talk to her. Sometimes in my imagination I think of her as my daughter—not by Jerry, of course—and I just wanted to shake her hand. I thought maybe after the show we'd hug. Is that asking too much?

THERAPIST: No.

ANNE: I bid on a dress of hers once at a charity auction. Somebody else outbid me, though. I wanted to go twenty dollars higher but Jerry said it's a used dress, we can get you a new one for less than that. Then, of course, we didn't. That's how things went with him.

THERAPIST: And he never brought you to orgasm.

ANNE: Well, I don't know about that.

THERAPIST: Yes you do.

132

ANNE: I might have had one and forgotten.

THERAPIST: You wouldn't forget.

ANNE: I think sex is overrated anyway. I can't imagine writing a whole book about it. What did you say?

THERAPIST: Have you ever just wanted to ram yourself into something?

ANNE: You know I have. Maybe I could read a chapter real fast. If only that wreck hadn't happened. Look, I'm still trembling.

THERAPIST: You can't read it in six minutes.

ANNE: Right, so tell me. I once heard my mother say it feels like a sneeze between your legs. Should I say that?

THERAPIST: Why don't you focus on the spiritual dimension of sex? Two human beings coming together, each giving their body over to the other, moving out of themselves into the other...

ANNE: It sounds like a head-on collision. *(Beat.)* I'm sorry. I'm wrong.

THERAPIST: No, you're right. It does.

ANNE: Both drivers died. The debris was so bad the ambulances almost hit each other. *(Beat.)* What was the wreck you saw?

THERAPIST: My husband and his girlfriend.

ANNE: Oh.

THERAPIST: He was sitting in the car on a country road waiting for her and she plowed into him at sixty miles an hour.

ANNE: Did they die?

THERAPIST: No, they both had airbags.

ANNE: Those things are amazing. I wish I could go through life wearing airbags in my clothes. I don't think they had airbags this morning. I don't have them, my car doesn't.

THERAPIST: Right after she hit his car she jumped out of hers screaming, "You can't do this to me. I love you. I thought you loved me." Can you imagine?

ANNE: Amazing.

THERAPIST: I can still hear her saying that. I remember thinking that was what I wanted to yell at him, and she'd taken that too.

ANNE: *(Touching the doctor gingerly.)* I'm sorry.

(Short silence.)

THERAPIST: Five minutes. This is awful.

ANNE: Tell me something to say. I wish I'd read the book. I really ought to read more.

THERAPIST: It has exercises you can do with your partner.

ANNE: But Jerry's dead!

THERAPIST: Maybe you could do them with Oprah.

ANNE: Sex exercises?

THERAPIST: No, it's just ways of developing intimacy, touching each other's inner selves.

ANNE: I already know her inner self. I watch her every day. I know every outfit she owns. I wonder if she's ever going to sell any more of her dresses.

THERAPIST: Why do you want one?

ANNE: Because I want to know what it feels like to be her. Maybe I'll never know what it's like to be rich or famous, but I could know what it feels like to step into the dress of a woman who's beautiful, who knows how to talk to people and how to listen to them. I'd zip her zipper up my back and feel her sleeves on my arms and close my eyes and just for a minute, I'd let myself pretend I was not just in her dress, I was in *her* and I'd become her and she'd become me. I want to do that before I die. *(Short silence.)* I think they died instantly. They would've had to. They were completely smashed together. You couldn't tell one car from the other.

THERAPIST: I would imagine.

ANNE: Jerry took several days. He went into a coma. He had tubes hooking him up to every kind of machine there is. It was awful. And then the trial lasted for months.

THERAPIST: Can we try to put that off for an hour, talk about it as soon as the show is over? Would you do that for me?

ANNE: I'm sorry, you're right, I'm obsessing.

THERAPIST: That's not what I said.

ANNE: You actually saw your husband's wreck happen?

THERAPIST: I told you.

ANNE: My heart was pounding so hard and so fast I could feel it all the way through my body and my skin went tight and hot and I had to fight to keep my eyes open and it was coming and coming, I knew what was going to happen, I knew. And then it did and I felt the impact in my teeth and the whole world was crashing noises and echoes of crashing noises and spinning and then I heard my voice, my own voice above all the clatter, and I realized I'd been screaming and I stopped. *(Beat.)* Is that how it was for you?

THERAPIST: I was hiding behind a tree. I had a camera with me and I was going to take pictures of them having sex and then I was going to divorce him, and when I saw her car coming, I saw what she was going to do, and I hoped he'd die.

ANNE: You were lucky.

(Therapist looks at her in a question.)

ANNE: I think if Jerry's girlfriend had tried to kill him, even if she'd failed, I could have gotten what I needed from that. Then I wouldn't have had to do it myself.

(Pause while therapist looks at her watch.)

THERAPIST: We can't talk about this right now. In two minutes…

ANNE: I know, I'm sorry.

THERAPIST: Don't talk about Jerry on the show.

ANNE: I promise.

THERAPIST: Not a word.

ANNE: Nothing.

THERAPIST: He never existed. You're just beginning therapy…

ANNE: I had therapy in jail.

THERAPIST: No, you never went to jail. You're a widow beginning private therapy and you're a typical postmenopausal woman in the sense that you have deep longings for human connection inside you that you don't know how to address because you haven't read my book, and I'm going to tell you what you should do, and you're going to sit there and say I'm right, okay?

ANNE: Okay.

THERAPIST: And after the show, right after you hug Oprah, we'll get in our cars and go to my office and we'll have a long session.

ANNE: We'll get in our cars.

THERAPIST: And go to my office.

ANNE: I don't have airbags.

THERAPIST: It's time to go.

ANNE: Do I look okay.

THERAPIST: You look beautiful. Right now, you're wearing the dress of a beautiful woman.

ANNE: Jerry was killed in a car crash. I ran into him with my car in the yard before I hit the house.

THERAPIST: It's okay.

ANNE: I wasn't trying to kill him. I was just trying to get him to listen to me. Afterwards I got out of the car and my head was bleeding so bad I could hardly see but I made my way over the bricks to him and I held him in my arms, my blood dripping on his face, and I said, "When this is all over, can we talk?"

THERAPIST: You and I, we'll talk.

ANNE: What did you do after the girlfriend yelled at your husband?

THERAPIST: I took pictures of them. Then I told them to go fuck themselves and filed for divorce.

ANNE: You look beautiful too.

THERAPIST: Come on.

ANNE: Do you have airbags?

THERAPIST: Yes.

If We Are Women

Joanna McClelland Glass

Scene: Guilford, CT

    2 Women: Rachel (60s) well-educated and acerbic and Ruth (60s) illiterate, open and unguarded.

Here, two very different grandmothers discover some common ground when their grand-daughter announces that she is in love.

        O   O   O

RUTH: I'll get on my knees tonight and pray that wee lass isn't pregnant.

RACHEL: Do you really believe someone listens?

RUTH: I do. I don't know why, because mostly He's tired and He's shut off his monitor. What about you?

RACHEL: I don't practice Judaism. I'm an agnostic.

RUTH: Agnostic. *(Thinking.)* Did Martin Luther start that one, too?

RACHEL: The word was introduced by a man called Thomas Huxley, in 1869. It means a…a…suspension of judgment in matters that can't be proved.

RUTH: I see. On the fence, then, about God.

RACHEL: Yes.

RUTH: What brought you to that conclusion?

RACHEL: When I was sixteen some cousins came over from Europe with terrible tales. Property being confiscated, Jews being rounded up and sent to work camps. I prayed mightily every day for a couple of years. Then I saw pictures of the death camps. Heaps of skeletons, gold from their teeth, their shoes, their spectacles. And just at that time I read one of Shakespeare's sonnets. He referred to *deaf heaven*. Deaf heaven not hearing his cries. I thought, yes, indeed. Deaf, blind, incapacitated heaven. I haven't prayed since.

RUTH: Are you Jewish at all, then?

RACHEL: The traditions are ingrained, and the antennae are always out. Sometimes I'll hear, from kids in an alley somewhere, *kike, yid, hebe*. You can be an agnostic, but you can't be on the fence when you hear those things.

RUTH: They hurt.

RACHEL: They are daggers to the heart.

(Rachel allows exposure. Ruth, very moved, tries to touch Rachel. Rachel tightens up and recoils at the prospect of being hugged.)

RACHEL: Excuse me. I'm sorry. That was a mawkish thing to say. *(A light goes on in Rachel. She remembers something, allowing for a quick change of subject.)* Estrous! That's it. Estrous. *(Running to write it down.)*

RUTH: Pardon?

RACHEL: When you used the term, *barnyard years*—I couldn't remember the word for it. The word that describes sexual frenzy. The estrous cycle is when the female mammal willingly accepts the male.

RUTH: Uh huh. I see a lot of estrous cycle on TV.

RACHEL: So do I.

RUTH: I thought you never watched.

RACHEL: From April 'till October, I live in my garden. Ruth, I think that if God is evident anywhere, it's in gardens. I watch TV occasionally in the winter, but I'm appalled at the sex and violence.

RUTH: All the real sex and violence is on the National Geographic animal shows.

RACHEL: Do you think so?

RUTH: I know so. There's a wild boar in Africa, a wild male boar whose penis is shaped like a corkscrew.

RACHEL: I saw that show! The penis was about six inches long, and it—*(Making a circling motion with her finger.)*—spiraled. I was amazed!

RUTH: I couldn't take my eyes off it.

RACHEL: *(Laughing.)* To be perfectly candid, neither could I.

Lady-Like
Laura Shamas

Scene: Wales, 1778
   3 Women: Lady Eleanor Butler (late 30s), Sarah Ponsonby (23) and Mary Carryll (30s); three young women who have escaped oppressive lives in Ireland.

Eleanor and Sarah have fled abusive homes along with Sarah's no-nonsense maid, Mary. Respite from the male-dominated world has presented itself in the form of a lovely cottage in Wales where the three friends determine to make a new life. Unfortunately, news of their scandalous flight has followed from Ireland, and here the three are shocked by an uncomplimentary article about them in the local paper.

MARY: Good God. A man was spying on us.

ELEANOR: *(Mocking.)* A man? Oh, no. Not a man, not one of those.

MARY: *(Pointing.)* See him a running down the hill. I'll go after him. *(She starts to exit.)* Stop, fool.

ELEANOR: Mary, wait. *(She detains Mary.)*

MARY: Let me get the kitchen knife. I'll change his mind about coming back.

ELEANOR: Let the ruffian go.

MARY: Then we'll start keeping a knife or two by our pillows. What's becoming of Wales? *(Mary takes the broom and exits into the house.)*

SARAH: Eleanor, perhaps I should go back to Ireland, to see about the annuity and visit my cousin.

ELEANOR: And admit to folly? We do not want all of Ireland gloating over our misfortune.

SARAH: Who would gloat now in the face of our failures?

ELEANOR: The Butlers. And then they'll know exactly where to find us.

SARAH: I am so homesick, Eleanor. Why can't we admit we were wrong and go back home?

ELEANOR: It takes time to build things, Sarah, whether it be home, hearth or a goodly soul. You should be more patient.

SARAH: There's no one more patient than I. At this rate, I'll be dead before I lose my patience.

(Mary enters from the kitchen carrying a copy of the General Evening Post.*)*

MARY: Excuse me, Ladies. I believe I know why we was being watched. *(She rustles the newspaper.)*

ELEANOR: Because of that? What's in there relating to us?

MARY: *(Reading aloud.)* "The Oldest Virgins in Wales. Extraordinary Female Affection."

(Sarah and Eleanor raise their eyebrows.)

SARAH: Things were going poorly. And now this.

MARY: *(Continued.)* "Miss Butler and Miss Ponsonby have retired from society into a certain Welch vale named Llangollen. Both Ladies are daughters of the great Irish families whose names they retain."

(Eleanor stands up.)

ELEANOR: What have you got there?

MARY: Today's *General Evening Post. (She continues reading.)* "Miss Butler, who is of the Ormonde family, had several offers of marriage, all of which she rejected. Miss Ponsonby, her particular friend and companion, was supposed to be the bar to any matrimonial union, so it was thought to separate them. Miss Butler was confined."

ELEANOR: *(Choked up.)* You're…reading this…from a newspaper?

MARY: It's quite extensive. It details your elopement.

SARAH: Where are the smelling salts? We're in the newspaper. The most horrible event of all.

ELEANOR: *(Grabbing the paper.)* "Miss Butler is tall and masculine. She wears always riding clothes. She hangs her black beaver's hat, usually worn by men, with the air of a sportsman in the hall, and appears in all respects a young man." *(She stops.)* These damn hats. "She does still retain a petticoat!" Has someone been watching us through the windows, seeing us dress?

SARAH: Smelling salts, smelling salts.

(Mary runs quickly into the house and fetches them. She places them under Sarah's nose. Sarah responds.)

ELEANOR: This is a total outrage. Listen to this. "Miss Ponsonby, on the contrary, is polite and effeminate, fair and beautiful. They live in neatness, elegance and taste. A female is their only servant. Miss Ponsonby does the duties and honors of the house while Miss Butler superintends the gardens and rest of the grounds. The two ladies share one small bed."

(Sarah starts to faint. Mary revives her with the smelling salts.)

MARY: We'll have onlookers dropping by for weeks, measuring your beds and watching for kisses. Just like the chap in the bushes.

ELEANOR: We shall cancel our subscription to this damnable garbage at once. *(Drops the newspaper.)*

SARAH: What to do, what to do.

ELEANOR: It makes us sound so unnatural. "The Oldest Virgins in Wales. Extraordinary Female Affection." I'll have this man's head. I'll write to a solicitor immediately.

SARAH: This paper circulates through all of England. My family is certain to get wind of this.

ELEANOR: The very idea that he's been creeping around, looking at us…

(A knock is heard. Mary rises.)

MARY: A caller. I'll see who it is.

ELEANOR: We can see no one.

(Mary nods and exits.)

SARAH: In eight months, we've had two callers. Now, on the eve of the greatest scandal of our lives, when we most need counsel, you say we can see no one.

ELEANOR: *(Holding newspaper.)* This destroys our retirement. Some traveler will carry this paper to Ireland and then we'll have no monies at all.

(Each has her own train of thought which is interrupted by the idea of the other. Yet each remains unresponsive.)

SARAH: All we wanted was to be left alone.

ELEANOR: Is news so scarce that privacy is invaded? Have they no one else of interest around here?

SARAH: I'm tired of isolation.

ELEANOR: The press is cheap. Maybe no one will pay attention to it.

SARAH: We're on the brink of disaster. We're in a headline.

ELEANOR: No one of importance will read such a rag.

SARAH: And you won't even take one visitor. Even dressed like this, so out of touch with fashion, I would withstand the humiliation just to welcome a new face.

(Mary returns with a card.)

MARY: Ladies, there's a gentleman here who demands to see you.

ELEANOR: Do we know him?

MARY: We do not. I have tried to discourage him from an interview with you at this time but he insists.

ELEANOR: The impudence! Who is this man?

MARY: A writer!

ELEANOR: Not another press scribe!

MARY: No, mum. Although he did read today's article, he assures me he's a poet.

SARAH: With our reputations on the line, we cannot be rude. We cannot turn him away. We must see him, to counteract this outrageous criminal report now tarnishing our good names.

ELEANOR: Why? So he can write a poem or something?

MARY: Poetry has rarely salvaged a woman's reputation.

ELEANOR: *(Tensely.)* We must remain calm.

SARAH: We must put on an air of calm and elegance. Pray what is this man's name?

MARY: *(Reading from card.)* "William Wordsworth."

ELEANOR: What a false-sounding name. Send him away, Mary.

SARAH: Yes, send him away. Send good Mr. Wordsworth away. Lady Eleanor has brushed him away with a flick of her wrist, in a show of her great power. Why is Lady Eleanor so afraid of receiving a man of letters, since she professes to be so inclined herself? Because she might find out she's not as smart as she thinks, in the face of a real, living, breathing bard. She writes on the sly—but will it measure up to the scrutiny of a true poet? She's not sure. So leave Lady Eleanor in our little utopian cocoon, where she's covered with your butterfly silk and mine, Mary. Who can stand a person who will not grow their own wings? Or will not let others? Go ahead, send him away. And as long as there's no sense of balance in this relation, I'll go away, too, and let you explain this to good Mr. Wordsworth, whoever he may be. Good-bye.

(Sarah exits. Eleanor and Mary exchange a look.)

ELEANOR: She can't leave. She'd never really go, would she?

MARY: She was quite serious. She's headed down the road. She even took her sketch pad.

ELEANOR: God. She's leaving. What will we say to this Mr. Wordsworth now?

A Pirate's Lullaby
Jessica Litwak

Scene: The high seas, 18th century

    2 Women: Anne Bonney (20s) an Irish pirate, fearless and outspoken and Mary Reade (20-30) an English pirate, courageous and spirited.

These two legendary buccaneers meet here for the first time when Mary joins the crew of Anne's ship disguised as a man.

O   O   O

(Anne approaches the boat and enters through the door to the deck where Mary is reading. The following scene is a dance of flirtation. The first chapter of a long love story.)

ANNE: Good book, Mr. Reade?

MARY: Not bad, *Mistress* Bonney.

ANNE: Serious fellow are ya?

MARY: Serious?

ANNE: Readin' books 'n all that. Must be very serious about life.

MARY: Not really. Reading relaxes me.

ANNE: That sort of relaxin' is mighty suspect, Mr. Reade. Doesn't go down well on a pirate ship.

MARY: What should I be doing, then?

ANNE: Drinking. Shouting. Singing. Fucking.

MARY: I see. Proper Pirate Behavior.

ANNE: That's right.

MARY: Well I'm a different sort of man.

ANNE: What sort of man is that?

MARY: Quiet.

ANNE: Strange.

MARY: Independent.

ANNE: Lonesome.

MARY: Clearheaded.

ANNE: Boring.

MARY: Sharp of sword.

ANNE: Pretty of face.

MARY: Strong willed.

ANNE: *(Touching her.)* Strong armed.

MARY: *(Pulling away.)* I'm my own man, Mistress Bonney.

ANNE: *(Moving toward him.)* I'm my own woman, Mr. Reade.

MARY: I hear you're Calico Jack's woman.

ANNE: I'm Anne Bonney's woman and no one's but.

MARY: Well good for you then that's as it should be.

ANNE: Like to dance?

MARY: Not at the moment, thank you.

ANNE: *(Mocking.)* Not at the moment thank you. You're a right stiff one, Mr. Reade. Lovely, though…

(Anne grabs Mary's arm.)

ANNE: Come on, give us a kiss.

MARY: No.

ANNE: Don't ya think I'm pretty?

MARY: You're very pretty…but I can't kiss you.

ANNE: Afraid of Jack then?

MARY: I can stand up to Jack Rackham with no trouble at all.

ANNE: What's wrong with ya then Mark Reade? Do ya prefer kissin' boys?

MARY: Don't run with that one. You'll turn the whole ship against me.

ANNE: Kiss me then.

MARY: Leave off, Bonney.

ANNE: Can't, mate. When I want somethin' I got to get it. And I lately have decided it's you that I want…more then all the rum in Jamaica…don't ya want me, bloke…even just a little?

MARY: No.

ANNE: No?

MARY: *Go away!*

ANNE: *No!*

(She grabs Mary and kisses her hard and long. They break away exhausted.)

ANNE: That was nice. Wasn't it?…

(Pause.)

MARY: Yes.

ANNE: Let's do it again!

MARY: No!

ANNE: Why not?

MARY: There's somethin' about me you don't realize.

ANNE: What's that, Mark?

MARY: Can't tell you…

ANNE: *(Interrupting.)* You don't have to be ashamed, Mark. If I were you, I'd be scared as well.

MARY: I'm not scared.

ANNE: You should be. Calico Jack has fed many a captive to the hungry fishies. Made 'em take a long walk home.

MARY: I'm not a captive. I'm a member of the crew.

ANNE: Don't matter a bit. If Jack decides he don't trust ya. He keelhauls men regular. Hangs 'em off the stern by a long rope and drags 'em back and forth under the ship. Once he took a juicy bite right out of a prisoner's heart. 'Nother time he wrapped the entire crew of a prize up in the mainsail and heaved it into the ocean.

MARY: You're full of shit, Anne Bonney. Trying to frighten me.

ANNE: Doing a good job of it as well.

MARY: I'm more experienced than you think.

ANNE: You've probably never even killed a man.

MARY: I've killed a man.

ANNE: So what's wrong with ya then? Why won't ya kiss me?

MARY: I've got privacies that need to be kept private. Secrets I can't tell. I want this job and I won't have you mucking it up for me now, before we've even left port…So go find yourself another little playmate Anne. It won't be me.
(Anne pauses for a moment, starts to leave.)

ANNE: You're sure then?

MARY: Very sure. Go away.
(Anne begins to leave then changes her mind and runs to embrace Mary.)

ANNE: Bollocks to that love. I'm hungry for ya.
(Between kisses, Mary trying to pull away…)

ANNE: I don't know what it is about ya, Mark, but there's somethin' familiar, somethin' delicious…
(She begins to unbutton Mary's shirt.)

MARY: Don't do that.

ANNE: Got to,…I'm mad in love with ya…
(Anne with one hand in Mary's shirt, makes a discovery and yelps, pulling her hand out fast.)

ANNE: You're…

MARY: A woman.

ANNE: Jesus.

MARY: Tried to warn you off.

ANNE: Who else knows?

MARY: No one but you.

ANNE: How long you been a bloke? I mean…dressing…

MARY: Mostly all my life. And you?

ANNE: Me? Since I was a boy. *You're* very good at it though.

MARY: Thank you.

ANNE: Who do you sleep with then? Women or…

MARY: *(Interrupting.)* No one these days, Anne. But the kiss was nice.

ANNE: Yeah, I could kill ya fur that.

MARY: Let's keep it between us then, shall we?

ANNE: You'll never get away with this.

MARY: I've gotten away with this for years. I've been a sailor, and a soldier as well.

ANNE: So why do ya want to be a pirate?

144

MARY: My father was before me. I don't know. It feels…Alive. Free.

ANNE: Ya won't feel very alive and free if I tell Jack you've got titties.

MARY: Are you going to tell Jack?

ANNE: I should tell him. Tell him everything. Shouldn't I?

MARY: Depends. Do you want to tell him?

ANNE: I dunno…

MARY: He'd throw me off.

ANNE: Or lock ya up in the hold.

MARY: Or lock me up.

ANNE: Or kill ya.

MARY: Or kill me.

(Pause.)

ANNE: I am the only girl on board ship ya know.

MARY: Yes, I know.

ANNE: It gets tiresome.

MARY: I can imagine.

ANNE: It might be good to have a secret.

MARY: And a friend?

ANNE: Yeah, maybe…and a friend…I'll think about it, Reade…Oh, what's your name? Not Mark…

MARY: Mary.

ANNE: Mary. Catholic even. Jesus. *(She moves away. Stops by the door.)* I'll promise ya this, Mary. I'll keep quiet today. I don't know about tomorrow.

MARY: We're sailing tonight. I'll be in deep trouble if you change your mind at high sea.

ANNE: Keep ya on your toes, pirate. *(She exits the deck and appears down below on the dock stage left.)* Oy, *Mark!*

MARY: Yes?

ANNE: Get drunk why don't ya? It's good form.

MARY: I appreciate the advice.

ANNE: And put away the book, it buggers the captain.

MARY: I understand.

ANNE: And Mark?

MARY: Yes?

ANNE: Nice kiss.

Twelve Dreams

James Lapine

Scene: A university town in New England, 1936
    2 Women: Emma (10) a young girl mourning the death of her mother, and Jenny (30-40) her father's housekeeper.

Lonely Emma is trying to make sense of her mother's death. Her father, a psychiatrist, has offered little emotional support. Here, Emma poses some difficult questions to Jenny, their pragmatic housekeeper.

$\bigcirc$ $\bigcirc$ $\bigcirc$

(Evening. New England, 1937. The bedroom of a ten-year-old girl, Emma. Her Irish housekeeper, Jenny, is with her.)

JENNY: Emma, let's get into bed.

EMMA: I'm trying to find Orion's belt.

JENNY: Emma…

EMMA: Do you think anyone lives in space?

JENNY: No, I don't.

EMMA: But isn't that where heaven is?

JENNY: No one's sure where heaven is.

EMMA: But if it's not in space, where is it Jenny?

JENNY: Emma, drink your milk.

EMMA: I don't think Daddy believes there is a heaven.

JENNY: Why not?

EMMA: When I told him you said that was where Mommy was, he said you didn't have that information.

JENNY: Emma! Bed.

EMMA: Okay. *(Gets into bed.)* Jenny, I have an itch on my back. Would you scratch it for me?

JENNY: You seem to always have an itch around this time.

EMMA: Please…

JENNY: Okay. *(Rubs her back.)*

EMMA: Jenny, did my mother dress like Miss Banton or Mrs. Trowbridge?

JENNY: Who is Mrs. Trowbridge?

EMMA: The fancy lady who visits Daddy.

JENNY: And how do you know her name?

EMMA: I heard it one day.

146

JENNY: *(Angry.)* You have big ears, young lady, and if you're not careful, some-body's going to snip them off! You know not to play near your father's study when he's working.

EMMA: I'm sorry.

JENNY: *(Cools down; continues to rub back.)* No. Your mother did not dress like either of them. She was a very stylish woman in her way. Not showy.

EMMA: Am I going to look like her?

JENNY: Well, you have your mother's eyes, and I think her smile, but in many ways you are your father's little girl.

EMMA: And what did Mother die from?

JENNY: She was very sick and she just died.

EMMA: Why do some people die and others don't?

JENNY: Emma, everyone dies. Some just die sooner than others.

EMMA: Did God make her die?

JENNY: *(Stops rubbing her back.)* Emma, I think you should have this discussion with your father. Now stop with your endless questions. *(Tucking her in.)* One thing is for sure. You have your father's mind.

EMMA: What kind of mind do you have, Jenny?

JENNY: At the moment, a very tired one. Now enough of this conversation. Say your prayers.

EMMA: Say them with me, Jenny.

(Music.)

JENNY: Spread out thy wings, Lord Jesus mild,

And take to thee thy chick, thy child

(Emma joins in.)

If Satan would devour it

No harm shall overpower it,

So let the angels sing!

JENNY: Sleep tight, Emma. Sweet dreams.

(She kisses her.)

EMMA: Good night, Jenny.

JENNY AND EMMA: Don't let the bedbugs bite!

Permission Acknowledgments

ATTENTION PERFORMERS: Permission is not required to use this material for audition and class study.

ALPHABET OF FLOWERS by Elyse Nass. Copyright © 1993 by Elyse Nass. Reprinted by permission of the author. All inquiries should be addressed to Elyse Nass, 59-15 47th Avenue, Woodside, NY 11377.

AMERICAN MEDEA by Silas Jones. Copyright ©1995 by Silas Jones. Reprinted by permission of the author. All inquiries should be addressed to Silas Jones, 642 Burnside Avenue, #2, Los Angeles, CA 90036.

BARKING SHARKS by Israel Horovitz. Copyright ©1995 by Israel Horovitz. Reprinted by permission of the author. All inquiries should be addressed to Mary Meagher, William Morris Agency, 1325 Avenue of the Americas, New York, NY 10019.

BEAST ON THE MOON by Richard Kalinoski. Copyright ©1995 by Richard Kalinoski. Reprinted by permission of the author. CAUTION: Professionals and amateurs are hereby warned that BEAST ON THE MOON by RICHARD KALINOSKI is subject to a royalty. It is fully protected under the copyright laws of the United States of America, and of all countries covered by the International Copyright Union (including the Dominion of Canada and the rest of the British Commonwealth), and of all countries covered by the Pan-American Copyright Convention and the Universal Copyright Convention, and of all countries with which the United States has reciprocal copyright relations. All rights, including professional, amateur, motion picture, recitation, lecturing, public reading, radio broadcasting, television, video or sound taping, all other forms of mechanical or electronic reproduction, such as information storage and retrieval systems and photocopying, and the rights of translation into a foreign language, are strictly reserved. Particular emphasis is laid upon the matter of readings, permission for which must be secured from the Author's agent in writing. Inquiries concerning rights should be addressed to the author's agent: Susan Schulman, A Literary Agency, 454 West 44th Street., New York, NY 10036.

BELOW THE BELT by Richard Dresser. ©1995 by Richard Dresser. Reprinted by permission of the author. All inquiries should be addressed to the author's agent, Mr. David Styne, Creative Artists Agency, 9830 Wilshire Blvd., Beverly Hills, CA 90212.

BLISS by Benjamin Bettenbender. Copyright © 1995 by Benjamin Bettenbender. Reprinted by permission of the author. All inquiries should be addressed to Bruce Ostler, Fifi Oscard Agency, 24 West 40th Street, New York, NY 10018.

BOCA by Christopher Kyle. Copyright ©1995 by Chistopher Kyle. Reprinted by permission of the author. All inquiries should be adressed to Helen Merrill Ltd., 435 West 23rd Street #1A, New York, NY 10011.

BY THE SEA: DUSK by Terrence McNally. Copyright ©1995 by Terrence McNally. Reprinted by permission of the author. All inquiries should be addressed to Gilbert Parker, William Morris Agency,1325 Avenue of the Americas, New York, NY 10019.

CLEAN by Edwin Sanchez. Copyright ©1994 by Edwin Sanchez. Reprinted by permission of the author. All inquiries should be addressed to Carl Mulert, The Joyce Ketay Agency, 1501 Broadway, Suite 1910, New York, NY 10036.

CLOUD TECTONICS by José Rivera. Copyright ©1995 by José Rivera. Reprinted by permission of the author. All inquiries should be addressed to Carl Mulert, The Joyce Ketay Agency, 1501 Broadway, Suite 1910, New York, NY 10036.

DANCE WITH ME by Jean Reynolds. Copyright ©1995 by Jean Reynolds. Reprinted by permission of the author. All inquiries should addressed to Jean Reynolds, 61 Morton Street, New York, NY 10014.

DATES AND NUTS by Gary Lennon. Copyright © 1995 by Gary Lennon. Reprinted by permission of William Craver. All inquiries should be addressed to William Craver, Writers and Artists Agency, 19 West 44th St. Suite 1000, New York, NY 10036.

148